The Song of Solomon

Concise Notes

(A *Concise Notes on the Bible* Series)

Stanford E. Murrell

A Divine Narrative
Setting Forth a Spiritual Drama of Love
Between
Christ and the Church
Illustrated in the Love of
Solomon for a Shulamite Maiden

Contents

SONG OF SOLOMON 1

Divine Author: God the Holy Spirit
Human Author: Solomon, King of Israel
Date of Writing: c. 965 BC - 926 BC
Statistics: 22nd book of the *Bible*, 8 chapters, 117 verses

Main Characters

- Solomon, a type of Christ
- The Shulamite maiden, a type of the church
- Two brothers
- The daughters of Jerusalem

The Story Behind the Song

According to *Song of Solomon 8:11*, king Solomon had a vineyard in the North Country in the mountain district of Ephraim. This vineyard was attended to by an Ephraimite family. If the mother and father were not dead they are not mentioned but at least two sons are for we read, *"My mother's children were angry with me" (SS 1:6)* or literally, *"My mother's sons."* In addition to at least the two sons there were two daughters, two sisters, a little one spoken of in Song 8: 8, *"We have a little sister."* And there was the older daughter, the Shulamite maiden. This older sister may not have been appreciated as much as she might have been. She was made to work hard in the vineyard. *"My mother's sons were angry with me,"* she said though not why.
"They made me the keeper of the vineyards; but mine own vineyard have I not kept."

The Shulamite maiden was responsible to prune the vines and set the traps for the little foxes that would come to spoil the vines by eating the grapes. She was also responsible for care for the lambs and the kids of the flock and if all that were not enough she had to protect and find an appropriate pasture for them. The Shulamite maiden worked hard in the sun from morning till dark. As a result she had no opportunity to cultivate a potential home of her own or take care of her own personal appearance. *"Mine own vineyard have I not kept."*

And there was something else which made the maiden sad. She could look out on those who passed by and see the beautiful ladies of the court riding in their finery. Then she looked at herself and reflected, *"I am black [dark], but comely [lovely]."* By self analysis the Shulamite maiden knew she could be fairly attractive even if she could not care for herself as much as she would have liked.

One day, in the providence of God a handsome stranger-shepherd came to her vineyard. His gaze was so tender and so intense upon her she felt forced to exclaim, *"Look not upon me, because I am black, because the sun hath looked upon me" (SS 1:6)*. Then she went on to explain why she had to work in the vineyard. *"My mother's children were angry with me; they made me the keeper of the vineyards; but mine own vineyard have I not kept."*

The stranger-shepherd responded to this anxious explanation with kindness. He did not think the maiden was sunburnt and unpleasant to look upon. He believed she was altogether lovely. For a young lady starved for affection and personal appreciation such a response would have been most welcomed and valued. In a moment of time the stranger-shepherd had won the heart of the shepherdess. Unfortunately, he could not linger but had to go away. However, it was his stated intention to return and make the Shulamite maiden his bride. Did she believe that? Indeed she did. Even when he became evasive in his answer as to where he fed his flock she trusted him. The stranger-shepherd went away and he was gone for a long period of time. Sometimes the Shulamite maiden would dream of him. She would awake to exclaim, *"The voice of my beloved,"* only to discover the silence of the darkness around her. Still she trusted his word.

One day the Shulamite maiden looked up and saw a great cloud of dust. People gathered to see what it meant for a thunderous cavalcade was approaching. The king's bodyguard was coming and the king himself. The royal entourage stopped at the vineyard of the Shulamite maiden. As promised the king had come for his bride. Now the Shulamite maiden could say outwardly for the entire world to hear, *"I am my beloveds, and his desire is toward me."*

In this lovely narrative the story of the relationship between Christ and the church is illustrated. Like the Shulamite maiden the church is in the world but not of it. Her heart is set on better things. Like the Shulamite maiden the church becomes the object of the King's love. While, the King must go away He will one day come again for His bride.

> "When He comes, the glorious King,
> All His ransomed home to bring,
> Then anew this song we'll sing,
> 'Hallelujah, what a Savior!'"

1 The Song of Songs, which is Solomon's.

1:1 Solomon (sol'-o-mun; peaceful), was the son of David and third king of Israel. Because of his sins, the kingdom of Israel was torn apart to form two separate nations. Despite his political troubles Solomon had a great capacity for personal love.

The Shulamite Maiden

2 Let him kiss me with the kisses of his mouth: for thy love [loving you] *is* better than wine.

1: 2 kiss me. As the Shulamite maiden expresses her delight in her stranger-shepherd so the believer can express love for Christ, the great Shepherd of the soul.

> "How sweet the name of Jesus sounds
> In a believer's ear!
> It soothes his sorrows,

> heals his wounds,
> And drives away his fear."

The Daughters of Jerusalem

3 Because of the savour of thy good ointments thy name is as ointment poured forth, therefore do the virgins love thee.

1:3 virgins. The reference is to the other maidens dwelling in the royal palace.

The Shulamite Maiden in the Court of the King

4 Draw me, we will run after thee: the king [Solomon] hath brought me into his chambers:

The Daughters of Jerusalem

we will be glad and rejoice in thee, we will remember thy love more than wine: the upright love thee.

1:4 brought me. At some point the Shulamite maiden was brought from the hill country into the royal palace or at least into the traveling royal chambers. She was drawn with cords of love as surely as every believer is drawn irresistibly to Christ.

> "I am Thine, O Lord,
> I have heard Thy voice,
> And it told Thy love to me;
> But I long to rise in the arms of faith,
> And be closer drawn to Thee.

> Draw me nearer, nearer, nearer,
> blessed Lord, To the Cross
> where Thou hast died;
> Draw me nearer, nearer, nearer,
> blessed Lord,
> To Thy precious bleeding side."

1:4 more than wine. Wine is used in *Scripture* as a symbol of joy because of its exhilarating nature. Wine can stimulate and cheer which is why the author of Proverbs said, *"Give strong drink unto him that is ready to perish, and wine unto those that be of heavy hearts. 7 Let him drink, and forget his poverty, and remember his misery no more" (Proverbs 31:6-7)*. Spiritually, the heart must learn to love Christ and be exhilarated by His love. There is indescribable joy in being occupied with the person of Christ.

> "Oh, how I love Jesus,
> Oh, how I love Jesus,

> Oh, how I love Jesus,
> Because He first loved me."
>
> The Lord does not want us to be drunk with wine but He would like for Christians to know the joy of His presence and the delight of His company. *Ephesians 5:18 And be not drunk with wine, wherein is excess; but be filled with the Spirit.*

The Shulamite Maiden
Remembers the Initial Meeting of her Stranger-Shepherd

5 I *am* black [dark], but comely [lovely], O ye daughters of Jerusalem, as the tents of Kedar, as the curtains of Solomon.

> 1:5 tents of Kedar. The Arab tents were made of black goat's hair.
>
> 1:5 as the curtains of Solomon. The Shulamite woman was as lovely as the curtains of Solomon which were known for their lavish beauty and intricate designs.

6 Look not upon me, because I am black, because the sun hath looked upon me: my mother's children were angry with me; they made me the keeper of the vineyards; *but* mine own vineyard have I not kept.

7 Tell me, O thou whom my soul loveth, where thou feedest, where thou makest *thy flock* to rest at noon: for why should I be as one that turneth aside by the flocks of thy companions?

> 1:7 Tell me... where thou feedest. Once love has been found, it never wants to let it go. When the disciples of John came to Jesus they asked Him, *"Master, where dwellest Thou?"* And He said, *"Come and see. They came and saw where he dwelt, and abode with him that day: for it was about the tenth hour"* (John 1:38, 39). Love found must not be lost.

The Kindness of King Solomon

8 If thou know not, O thou fairest among women, go thy way forth by the footsteps of the flock, and feed thy kids beside the shepherds' tents.

9 I have compared thee, O my love, to a company of horses in Pharaoh's chariots.

10 Thy cheeks are comely [lovely] with rows *of jewels*, thy neck with chains *of gold*.

11 We will make thee borders of gold with studs of silver.

The Shulamite Maiden in Communion with the King

12 While the king *sitteth* at his table, my spikenard [perfume] sendeth forth the smell thereof.

13 A bundle of myrrh is my well beloved unto me; he shall lie all night betwixt my breasts.

1:12-13 my well beloved. The king and his bride are in the royal palace where they can have sweet communion and intimate expressions of love. And so it is that as the church enters into sweet communion with Christ there are depths of spiritual intimacy to be enjoyed. But let the church hear again. There can be no real communion, there can be no intimate worship except the heart is occupied with Christ. Good works and active service are no substitute for worship, adoration and praise. God has said, *"Whoso offereth praise glorifieth Me" (Psa. 50:23).* Even though the church has not seen Christ except by the eye of faith yet it must still love and worship Him. *"Whom having not seen, ye love; in whom, though now ye see him not, yet believing, ye rejoice with joy unspeakable and full of glory" (1 Peter 1:8).*

14 My beloved *is* unto me as a cluster of camphire [henna flowers] in the vineyards of Engedi.

1:14 beloved. This word is used 32 times in the books, always with a reference to Solomon. In like manner let the church speak of her Beloved often.

King Solomon Speaks

15 Behold, thou *art* fair, my love; behold, thou *art* fair; thou *hast* doves' eyes.

1:15 dove's eyes. Beautiful and gentle.

The Shulamite Maiden

16 Behold, thou art fair, my beloved, yea, pleasant: also our bed [couch] is green.

17 The beams of our house *are* cedar, *and* our rafters of fir.

1:15-17 Behold. In a fine house of cedar and fir the king speaks of the loveliness of his bride. To him she is altogether lovely. In like manner, in mansions of glory Christ sees the church as precious and priceless and worth dying for. He will one day present the church *"to himself a glorious church, not having spot, or wrinkle, or any such thing; but that it should be holy and without blemish" (Ephesians 5:27).*

Doctrine of Anger

1. The word *"anger"* means literally *"to breathe hard."*

2. Anger is a God given emotion to be used righteously.

   - *Ephesians 4:26 Be ye angry, and sin not: let not the sun go down upon your wrath: John 7:24 Judge not according to the appearance, but judge righteous judgment.*

1. Some anger is justified.

2. God the Father is angry with presumptuous sinning.

   - *Psalms 7:11 God judgeth the righteous, and God is angry with the wicked every day.*

3. God the Son is angry at the hardness of the human heart.

   - *Mark 3:5 And when he had looked round about on them with anger, being grieved for the hardness of their hearts, he saith unto the man, Stretch forth thine hand. And he stretched it out: and his hand was restored whole as the other.*

4. Moses was angry at the constant complaining of the children of Israel.

   - *Numbers 20:11 And Moses lifted up his hand, and with his rod he smote the rock twice: and the water came out abundantly, and the congregation drank, and their beasts also. 12 And the LORD spake unto Moses and Aaron, Because ye believed me not, to sanctify me in the eyes of the children of Israel, therefore ye shall not bring this congregation into the land which I have given them.*

5. Most anger is not productive. It does no good.

6. Wives are not to provoke their husbands.

   - *1 Peter 3:1 Likewise, ye wives, be in subjection to your own husbands; that, if any obey not the word, they also may without the word be won by the conversation of the wives; 2 While they behold your chaste conversation coupled with fear. 3 Whose adorning let it not be that outward adorning of plaiting the hair, and of wearing of gold, or of putting on of apparel; 4 But let it be the hidden man of the heart, in that which is not corruptible, even the ornament of a meek and quiet spirit, which is in the sight of God of great price. 5 For after this manner in the old time the holy women also, who trusted in God, adorned themselves, being in subjection unto their own husbands: 6 Even as Sara obeyed Abraham, calling him lord: whose daughters ye are, as long as ye do well, and are not afraid with any amazement.*

7. Husbands are not to provoke their wives.

   - *1 Peter 3:7 Likewise, ye husbands, dwell with them according to knowledge, giving honour unto the wife, as unto the weaker vessel, and as being heirs together of the grace of life; that your prayers be not hindered.*

8. Parents are not to provoke their children.

   - *Colossians 3:21 Fathers, provoke not your children to anger, lest they be discouraged.*

9. Employers are to treat their employees fairly and not provoke them.

   - *Ephesians 6:9 And, ye masters, do the same things unto them, forbearing threatening: knowing that your Master also is in heaven; neither is there respect of persons with him.*

10. Christians are not to provoke one another to anger through competition. *Gal 5:26 Let us not be desirous of vain glory, provoking one another, envying one another.*

11. Anger expresses itself in inappropriate actions or words.

    - Physical violence
    - Libel, which is writing something down which is not true with the intent to hurt someone's livelihood or reputation
    - Slander, which is unspoken truth or embellishment of the reason for one's anger
    - Maligning or taking the opportunity to let many others know what has been said or done
    - Railing (venting)

12. In the life of the believer illegitimate anger is to be put away.

    - *Ephesians 4:26 Be ye angry, and sin not: let not the sun go down upon your wrath:*

    - *Ephesians 4:31 Let all bitterness, and wrath, and anger, and clamour, and evil speaking, be put away from you, with all malice:*

13. One reason Christians should seek to put away anger is a desire to reflect the divine attribute of patience and grace.

    - *Psalms 103:8 The LORD is merciful and gracious, slow to anger, and plenteous in mercy.*

14. A person who is patient with others can make strife to cease.

    - *Proverbs 15:18 A wrathful man stirreth up strife: but he that is slow to anger appeaseth strife.*

15. The ability to control one's emotions is considered to be of greater value than a military victory.

    - *Proverbs 16:32 He that is slow to anger is better than the mighty; and he that ruleth his spirit than he that taketh a city.*

16. No one has to get angry. Anger is a matter of the will.

    - *Proverbs 19:11 The discretion of a man deferreth his anger; and it is his glory to pass over a transgression.*

17. Angry people do not make good friends.

    - *Proverbs 22:24 Make no friendship with an angry man; and with a furious man thou shalt not go:*

18. The sin of anger leads to other sins.

- *Proverbs 29:22 An angry man stirreth up strife, and a furious man aboundeth in transgression.*

19. An angry person is a foolish person.

   - *Ecclesiastes 7:9 Be not hasty in thy spirit to be angry: for anger resteth in the bosom of fools.*

20. It is foolish to make others angry.

   - *Proverbs 20:2 The fear of a king is as the roaring of a lion: whoso provoketh him to anger sinneth against his own soul.*

21. Most anger is unjustified.

   - The anger of Cain was unjustified. *1 John 3:12 Not as Cain, who was of that wicked one, and slew his brother. And wherefore slew he him? Because his own works were evil, and his brother's righteous.*

   - The anger of James and John was unjustified. *Luke 9:54 And when his disciples James and John saw this, they said, Lord, wilt thou that we command fire to come down from heaven, and consume them, even as Elias did?*

   - The anger of the Apostle Paul against Barnabas was unjustified. *Acts 15:39 And the contention was so sharp between them, that they departed asunder one from the other: and so Barnabas took Mark, and sailed unto Cyprus.*

   - The anger of Jonah against God for sparing the citizens of Nineveh was unjustified. *Jonah 4:4 Then said the LORD, Doest thou well to be angry?*

   - The stubborn heart will justify anger. *Jonah 4:9 And God said to Jonah, Doest thou well to be angry for the gourd? And he said, I do well to be angry, even unto death.*

22. Those who do not put away unlawful anger are in danger of eternal judgment.

   - *Matthew 5:22 But I say unto you, That whosoever is angry with his brother without a cause shall be in danger of the judgment: and whosoever shall say to his brother, Raca, shall be in danger of the council: but whosoever shall say, Thou fool, shall be in danger of hell fire.*

23. One of the qualifications for useful spiritual service is to have a temperament that is void of excessive anger.

   - *Titus 1:7 For a bishop must be blameless, as the steward of God; not self-willed, not soon angry, not given to wine, no striker, not given to filthy lucre;*

24. God's anger can be deferred.

   - *Isaiah 48:9 For my name's sake will I defer mine anger, and for my praise will I refrain for thee, that I cut thee not off.*

25. The anger of the Lord is treasured up against the ungodly.

- *2 Peter 3:7 But the heavens and the earth, which are now, by the same word are kept in store, reserved unto fire against the day of judgment and perdition of ungodly men.*

26. God's anger is turned away by repentance

   - *Jeremiah 3:12 Go and proclaim these words toward the north, and say, Return, thou backsliding Israel, saith the LORD; and I will not cause mine anger to fall upon you: for I am merciful, saith the LORD, and I will not keep anger for ever.*

27. The anger of man is turned away by a soft answer and by doing something in secret for someone.

   - *Proverbs 15:1 A soft answer turneth away wrath: but grievous words stir up anger.*

   - *Proverbs 21:14 A gift in secret pacifieth anger….*

Parallels Between the Shulamite Maiden and the Church

1. The Shulamite maiden desired the kisses of Solomon as the Church should desire and seek an intimate relationship with Christ.

   - *Song of Solomon 1:2 Let him kiss me with the kisses of his mouth: for thy love is better than* wine.

2. The Shulamite maiden thought of herself in humble terms so the church must know humility.

   - *Song of Solomon 1:5 I am black, but comely, O ye daughters of Jerusalem, as the tents of Kedar, as the curtains of Solomon.*

   - *1 Peter 5:5 Likewise, ye younger, submit yourselves unto the elder. Yea, all of you be subject one to another, and be clothed with humility: for God resisteth the proud, and giveth grace to the humble.*

3. The Shulamite maiden desired to dwell with Solomon as the church should desire to dwell with Christ.

   - *Song of Solomon 1:7 Tell me, O thou whom my soul loveth, where thou feedest, where thou makest thy flock to rest at noon: for why should I be as one that turneth aside by the flocks of thy companions?*

   - *John 1:38 Then Jesus turned, and saw them following, and saith unto them, What seek ye? They said unto him, Rabbi, (which is to say, being interpreted, Master,) where dwellest thou?*

4. The Shulamite maiden found herself esteem in the presence and view of Solomon. The church finds her glory in the person of Christ.

   - *Song of Solomon 2:1 I am the rose of Sharon, and the lily of the valleys.*

   - *Revelation 21:2 And I John saw the holy city [the church], New Jerusalem, coming down from God out of heaven, prepared as a bride adorned for her husband.*

5. The Shulamite maiden found her security in the shadow of Solomon. The church finds her security in the body of Christ.

- *Song of Solomon 2:3 As the apple tree among the trees of the wood, so is my beloved among the sons. I sat down under his shadow with great delight, and his fruit was sweet to my taste.*

- *John 10:27 My sheep hear my voice, and I know them, and they follow me: 28 And I give unto them eternal life; and they shall never perish, neither shall any man pluck them out of my hand. 29 My Father, which gave them me, is greater than all; and no man is able to pluck them out of my Father's hand. 30 I and my Father are one.*

6. The Shulamite maiden enjoyed being under the banner of Solomon's love. The church is covered by the blood of Christ, the greatest banner of love.

- *Song of Solomon 2:4 He brought me to the banqueting house, and his banner over me was love.*

- *1 Peter 1:18 Forasmuch as ye know that ye were not redeemed with corruptible things, as silver and gold, from your vain conversation received by tradition from your fathers; 19 But with the precious blood of Christ, as of a lamb without blemish and without spot:*

7. The Shulamite maiden enjoyed the voice of her beloved as the church knows and enjoys the voice of Christ.

- *Song of Solomon 2:8 The voice of my beloved! Behold, he cometh leaping upon the mountains, skipping upon the hills.*

- *John 10:27 My sheep hear my voice, and I know them, and they follow me:*

8. The Shulamite maiden was concerned about the little foxes that would spoil the vines. The church must be concerned about any sin that would hurt the cause of Christ.

- *Song of Solomon 2:15 Take us the foxes, the little foxes, that spoil the vines: for our vines have tender grapes.*

- *Hebrews 12:1 Wherefore seeing we also are compassed about with so great a cloud of witnesses, let us lay aside every weight, and the sin which doth so easily beset us, and let us run with patience the race that is set before us,*

9. The Shulamite maiden sought and found Solomon and would not let him go. In like manner the church must seek Christ and never let Him go as Jacob wrestled with the Lord until the dawning of the day.

- *Song of Solomon 3:4 It was but a little that I passed from them, but I found him whom my soul loveth: I held him, and would not let him go, until I had brought him into my mother's house, and into the chamber of her that conceived me.*

- *Genesis 32:26 …And he [Jacob] said [to the Angel of the Lord], I will not let thee go , except thou bless me.*

10. The Shulamite maiden looked upon Solomon as someone to be desired above all others. So the Church looks at Christ as someone to be desired more than silver or gold.

"Jesus is all the world to me,
my life, my joy, my all;
He is my strength from day to day,
without Him I would fall.

When I am sad, to Him I go,
no other one can cheer me so;
When I am sad, He makes me glad,
He's my Friend.

Jesus is all the world to me,
my Friend in trials sore;
I go to Him for blessings,
and He gives them over and o'er.

He sends the sunshine and the rain,
He sends the harvest's golden grain;
Sunshine and rain, harvest of grain, He's my Friend.

Jesus is all the world to me,
and true to Him I'll be;
O how could I this Friend deny,
when He's so true to me?

Following Him I know I'm right,
He watches o'er me day and night;
Following Him by day and night,
He's my Friend.

Jesus is all the world to me,
I want no better Friend;
I trust Him now,
I'll trust Him when life's fleeting days shall end.

Beautiful life with such a Friend, beautiful life that has no end;
Eternal life, eternal joy, He's my Friend."

Will L. Thompson, 1904

11. The Shulamite maiden lost sight of her beloved. It is possible for the church to lose sight of Christ and go through a dark night of the soul.

   • *Song of Solomon 3:1 By night on my bed I sought him whom my soul loveth: I sought him, but I found him not.*

   • *Revelation 2:4 Nevertheless I have somewhat against thee, because thou hast left thy first love.*

12. The Shulamite woman made every effort to restore fellowship with the Lord. So the church must make every effort to restore fellowship with Christ if sin has broken that fellowship.

- *Song of Solomon 3:2 I will rise now, and go about the city in the streets, and in the broad ways I will seek him whom my soul loveth: I sought him, but I found him not.*

- *Revelation 3:20 Behold, I stand at the door, and knock: if any man hear my voice, and open the door, I will come in to him, and will sup with him, and he with me.*

Parallels Between the Solomon and Christ

1. Solomon was a singer of songs. So Christ was a singer of songs as well.

   - *Song of Solomon 1:1 The song of songs, which is Solomon's.*

   - *Matthew 26:30 And when they had sung an hymn, they went out into the Mount of Olives.*

2. The name of Solomon was precious to the Shulamite maiden. The name of Christ is above every name.

   - *Song of Solomon 1:3 Because of the savour of thy good ointments thy name is as ointment poured forth, therefore do the virgins love thee. Philippians 2:10 That at the name of Jesus every knee should bow, of things in heaven, and things in earth, and things under the earth; 11 And that every tongue should confess that Jesus Christ is Lord, to the glory of God the Father.*

3. Solomon brought his bride into his chambers. So Christ will bring His bride into His mansions.

   - *Song of Solomon 1:4 Draw me, we will run after thee: the king hath brought me into his chambers: we will be glad and rejoice in thee, we will remember thy love more than wine: the upright love thee.*

   - *John 14:1 Let not your heart be troubled: ye believe in God, believe also in me. 2 In my Father's house are many mansions: if it were not so, I would have told you. I go to prepare a place for you. 3 And if I go and prepare a place for you, I will come again, and receive you unto myself; that where I am, there ye may be also.*

4. Solomon viewed the Shulamite maiden in her bodily perfection as Christ views the Church as being without spot or blemish.

   - *Song of Solomon 1:10 Thy cheeks are comely with rows of jewels, thy neck with chains of gold. ....13 A bundle of myrrh is my wellbeloved unto me; he shall lie all night betwixt my breasts....15 Behold, thou art fair, my love; behold, thou art fair; thou hast doves' eyes.*

   - *Ephesians 5:25 ...Christ also loved the church, and gave himself for it; 26 That he might sanctify and cleanse it with the washing of water by the word, 27 That he might present it to himself a glorious church, not having spot, or wrinkle, or any such thing; but that it should be holy and without blemish .*

5. Solomon displayed his royalty. One day Christ will manifest the fact He is King of kings and Lord of lords. One day every knee shall bow to Him.

- *Song of Solomon 3:9 King Solomon made himself a chariot of the wood of Lebanon. 10 He made the pillars thereof of silver, the bottom thereof of gold, the covering of it of purple, the midst thereof being paved with love, for the daughters of Jerusalem. Romans 14:11 For it is written, As I live, saith the Lord, every knee shall bow to me, and every tongue shall confess to God.*

SONG OF SOLOMON 2

The Shulamite Maiden

1 I *am* the rose of Sharon, *and* the lily of the valleys.

> 2:1 Sharon, Plain of, refers to the Palestinian coastal plain between Joppa and Mount Carmel. It was about 50 miles long, 9 miles wide and was known for its beauty, pasturage, and fertility. The rose of Sharon refers specifically to the narcissus, a blood-red flower.
>
> 2:1 lily. The reference is to the beautifully flowering cyclamen. It is a well known and common pot plant with several pink flowers. The cyclamen is able to grow under deciduous or coniferous trees. It can grow in loose earth as well as hollow trees.

Solomon

2 As the lily among thorns, so *is* my love among the daughters.

> 2:2 thorns. The thorn speaks of those who are still under the curse while the lily speaks of those who have been redeemed and made precious in the sight of God. Though the church is still in the world and subject to its environment the church is special and fundamentally different.

The Shulamite Maiden

3 As the apple tree among the trees of the wood, so *is* my beloved among the sons. I sat down under his shadow with great delight, and his fruit was sweet to my taste.

> 2:3 apple tree. The Shulamite maiden looked upon Solomon as someone to be desired above all others. So the Church looks at Christ as someone to be desired above the world the flesh and the devil. *Psalms 37:4 Delight thyself also in the LORD; and he shall give thee the desires of thine heart.*

4 He brought me to the banqueting house, and his banner [flag] over me *was* love.

5 Stay me with flagons [raisin cakes], comfort me with apples: for I am sick [faint] of love.

6 His left hand *is* under my head, and his right hand doth embrace me.

7 I charge you [put you on an oath], O ye daughters of Jerusalem, by the roes, and by the hinds of the field, that ye stir not up, nor awake *my* love, till he please [until it is proper].

2:7 he pleases. A better translation gives the meaning that love is not to be disturbed until it is proper to do so. Once, when Mary was worshipping at the feet of Jesus, her sister Martha rebuked her for not doing other household chores. Jesus came to the defense of Mary and said in essence, *"Do not disturb love until it is proper to do so."* Mary had chosen to be close to Christ (Luke 10:41, 42).

The Shulamite Maiden the Expectation of Love

8 The voice of my beloved! Behold, he cometh leaping upon the mountains, skipping upon the hills.

9 My beloved is like a roe or a young hart: behold, he standeth behind our wall, he looketh forth at the windows, shewing himself through the lattice.

2:9 like a roe or a young hart. The symbolism is that of physical strength, masculine behavior and grace of movement.

The Shulamite Maiden quoting Solomon

10 My beloved spake, and said unto me, Rise up, my love, my fair one, and come away.

11 For, lo, the winter is past, the rain is over *and* gone;

12 The flowers appear on the earth; the time of the singing *of birds* is come, and the voice of the turtle [turtledove] is heard in our land;

13 The fig tree putteth forth her green figs, and the vines *with* the tender grape give a *good* smell. Arise, my love, my fair one, and come away.

"A little while'—the Lord shall come,
And we shall wander here no more;
He'll take us to His Father's home,
Where He for us is gone before—
To dwell with Him, to see His face,
And sing the glories of His grace."

Solomon

14 O my dove, *that art* in the clefts of the rock, in the secret *places* of the stairs, let me see thy countenance, let me hear thy voice; for sweet *is* thy voice, and thy countenance *is* comely.

2:13 clefts of the rock.

"A wonderful Savior is Jesus my Lord,
A wonderful Savior to me;
He hideth my soul in the cleft of the rock,
Where rivers of pleasure I see.

He hideth my soul in the cleft of the rock
That shadows a dry, thirsty land;
He hideth my life
with the depths of His love,
And covers me there with His hand,
And covers me there with His hand.

A wonderful Savior is Jesus my Lord,
He taketh my burden away;
He holdeth me up,
and I shall not be moved,
He giveth me strength as my day.

With numberless blessings
each moment He crowns,
And filled with His fullness divine,
I sing in my rapture, oh, glory to God
For such a Redeemer as mine!

When clothed in His brightness, transported I rise
To meet Him in clouds of the sky,
His perfect salvation, His wonderful love
I'll shout with the millions on high."

Fanny Crosby

The Daughters of Jerusalem

15 Take us the foxes, the little foxes, that spoil the vines: for our vines *have* tender grapes.

2:15. the foxes. The little foxes were known to do great damage to the vineyards. The plea is to not let little matters damage a beautiful relationship.

The Little Foxes of the Christian Life

- Spiritual carelessness
- Worldliness
- Unmortified sin
- Unconfessed sin
- Neglect of the Bible
- Neglect of prayer
- Neglect of meditation
- Neglect of the church

The Shulamite Maiden

16 My beloved *is* mine, and I *am* his: he feedeth among the lilies.

2:16 and I am his. The Doctrine of Eternal Security is not designed to produce careless living but to have tremendous confidence of an abiding love that will never let a person go.

17 Until the day break, and the shadows flee away, turn, my beloved, and be thou like a roe or a young hart upon the mountains of Bether [division].

2:17 Bether (be'-thur; dissection, separation, cutting), refers to a mountain range named in the Song of Solomon. It may be the same as the mountains of spice (Song of Solomon 8:14). The Shulamite maiden pleads that the mountain of separation might be dissolved.

Doctrine of the Shadow

1. In the hot eastern climate with the tropical sun burning down upon a traveler, a place of refuge from the scorching heat is welcomed.

2. A physical place of comfort speaks of spiritual truths.

   - *Psalms 17:8 Keep me as the apple of the eye, hide me under the shadow of thy wings,*

   - *Psalms 36:7 How excellent is thy loving-kindness, O God! Therefore the children of men put their trust under the shadow of thy wings.*

   - *Isaiah 32:2 And a man shall be as an hiding place from the wind, and a covert from the tempest; as rivers of water in a dry place, as the shadow of a great rock in a weary land.*

3. Time itself is but a shadow of things to come.

- *1 Chronicles 29:15 For we are strangers before thee, and sojourners, as were all our fathers: our days on the earth are as a shadow, and there is none abiding.*

- *Job 8:9 (For we are but of yesterday, and know nothing, because our days upon earth are a shadow :)*

4. Death is called a shadow and not something to be feared. The shadow of a dog cannot bite and the shadow of a candle cannot burn. So the shadow of death need hold no fear for the Christian.

- *Psalms 23:4 Yea, though I walk through the valley of the shadow of death, I will fear no evil: for thou art with me; thy rod and thy staff they comfort me.*

5. Despite the ravening effects of the Fall upon creation, it is no small mercy of God to provide a shadow of refuge for His creation.

- *Mark 4:32 [Jesus spoke of a small seed when planted.] But when it is sown, it groweth up, and becometh greater than all herbs, and shooteth out great branches; so that the fowls of the air may lodge under the shadow of it.*

6. To establish apostolic authority the shadow of Peter produced healing power.

- *Acts 5:15 Insomuch that they brought forth the sick into the streets, and laid them on beds and couches, that at the least the shadow of Peter passing by might overshadow some of them.*

7. The Mosaic Law with its rules and regulations was only a shadow of great gospel spiritual truths.

- *Colossians 2:16 Let no man therefore judge you in meat, or in drink, or in respect of an holyday, or of the new moon, or of the sabbath days: 17 Which are a shadow of things to come; but the body is of Christ.*

- *Hebrews 10:1 For the law having a shadow of good things to come, and not the very image of the things, can never with those sacrifices which they offered year by year continually make the comers thereunto perfect.*

8. While a physical shadow can offer rest and comfort a mental or spiritual shadow can obscure reality or a great truth. Only in God is there no shadow of this nature.

- *James 1:17 Every good gift and every perfect gift is from above, and cometh down from the Father of lights, with whom is no variableness, neither shadow of turning.*

Doctrine of Eternal Security

1. The Bible declares that once a person is saved or born again the soul is always saved.

2. The work of God the Father, God the Son and God the Holy Spirit guarantees the security of the believer.

3. The Father works for the salvation of souls for salvation is His plan and program.

    - *Romans 8:28 And we know that all things work together for good to them that love God, to them who are the called according to his purpose. 29 For whom he did foreknow, he also did predestinate to be conformed to the image of his Son, that he might be the firstborn among many brethren. 30 Moreover whom he did predestinate, them he also called: and whom he called, them he also justified: and whom he justified, them he also glorified.*

    - *Ephesians 1:3 Blessed be the God and Father of our Lord Jesus Christ, who hath blessed us with all spiritual blessings in heavenly places in Christ: 4 According as he hath chosen us in him before the foundation of the world, that we should be holy and without blame before him in love: 5 Having predestinated us unto the adoption of children by Jesus Christ to himself, according to the good pleasure of his will, 6 To the praise of the glory of his grace, wherein he hath made us accepted in the beloved. 7 In whom we have redemption through his blood, the forgiveness of sins, according to the riches of his grace; 8 Wherein he hath abounded toward us in all wisdom and prudence; 9 Having made known unto us the mystery of his will, according to his good pleasure which he hath purposed in himself: 10 That in the dispensation of the fullness of times he might gather together in one all things in Christ, both which are in heaven, and which are on earth; even in him: 11 In whom also we have obtained an inheritance, being predestinated according to the purpose of him who worketh all things after the counsel of his own will.*

    - *Ephesians 2:7 That in the ages to come he might shew the exceeding riches of his grace in his kindness toward us through Christ Jesus.*

4. The features of the Fathers plan of salvation are distinct.

5. The Father has predestinated [marked out beforehand] all those He foreknew [loved with an intimate love] to be conformed to the image of Christ.

    - *Romans 8:29 For whom he did foreknow, he also did predestinate to be conformed to the image of his Son, that he might be the firstborn among many brethren.*

6. The Father has accepted all those whom He has pre-determined to receive eternal life to be in Christ.
    - *Ephesians 1:6 To the praise of the glory of his grace, wherein he hath made us accepted in the beloved.*

    - *Colossians 3:3 For ye are dead, and your life is hid with Christ in God.*

7. The believer has as much right to be in heaven as Christ does, for he is in Christ.

8. The Father has planned to call, justify, and glorify all those appointed to be accepted in Christ.

    - *Romans 8:30 Moreover whom he did predestinate, them he also called: and whom he called, them he also justified: and whom he justified, them he also glorified.*

9. Glorification will take place at the Second Advent of Christ.

- *1 Corinthians 15:51 Behold, I shew you a mystery; We shall not all sleep, but we shall all be changed, 52 In a moment, in the twinkling of an eye, at the last trump: for the trumpet shall sound, and the dead shall be raised incorruptible, and we shall be changed. 53 For this corruptible must put on incorruption, and this mortal must put on immortality. 54 So when this corruptible shall have put on incorruption, and this mortal shall have put on immortality, then shall be brought to pass the saying that is written, Death is swallowed up in victory.*

10. In Romans 8:30 Paul puts the word in the past tense because in God's sight the believer is *already* glorified in heaven with Christ. This is the strongest verse in the Bible on eternal security.

11. The Father will gather together all those in Christ in the fullness of time.

- *Ephesians 1:10 That in the dispensation of the fullness of times he might gather together in one all things in Christ, both which are in heaven, and which are on earth; even in him.*

12. The Father will one day display those He has gathered in Christ as trophies of His grace throughout eternity.

- *Ephesians 2:7 That in the ages to come he might shew the exceeding riches of his grace in his kindness toward us through Christ Jesus.*

13. The security of the believer is assured because of the power of the Father.
- *John 10:29 My Father, which gave them me, is greater than all; and no man is able to pluck them out of my Father's hand.*

- *Romans 4:21 And being fully persuaded that, what he had promised, he was able also to perform.*

- *1 Corinthians 1:8 Who shall also confirm you unto the end, that ye may be blameless in the day of our Lord Jesus Christ. 9 God is faithful, by whom ye were called unto the fellowship of his Son Jesus Christ our Lord. (cf. Ephesians 3:20; Philippians 1:6; 2 Timothy 1:12; 4:18; Hebrews 7:25; 1 Peter 1:5; Jude 24).*

14. The security of the believer is assured because of the love of the Father.

- *Romans 5:7 For scarcely for a righteous man will one die: yet peradventure for a good man some would even dare to die. 8 But God commendeth his love toward us, in that, while we were yet sinners, Christ died for us. 9 Much more then, being now justified by his blood, we shall be saved from wrath through him. 10 For if, when we were enemies, we were reconciled to God by the death of his Son, much more, being reconciled, we shall be saved by his life. 11 And not only so, but we also joy in God through our Lord Jesus Christ, by whom we have now received the atonement.*

- *Romans 8:31 What shall we then say to these things? If God be for us, who can be against us? 32 He that spared not his own Son, but delivered him up for us all, how shall he not with him also freely give us all things? 33 Who shall lay any thing to the charge of God's elect? It is God that justifieth.*

15. The security of the believer is assured because of the faithfulness of the Father.

- *Hebrews 12:2 Looking unto Jesus the author and finisher of our faith; who for the joy that was set before him endured the cross, despising the shame, and is set down at the right hand of the throne of God. 3 For consider him that endured such contradiction of sinners against himself, lest ye be wearied and faint in your minds.*

16. The security of the believer is assured because of the Father's faithfulness in chastening His own Son.

- *Hebrews 12: 4 Ye have not yet resisted unto blood, striving against sin.5 And ye have forgotten the exhortation which speaketh unto you as unto children, My son, despise not thou the chastening of the Lord, nor faint when thou art rebuked of him: 6 For whom the Lord loveth he chasteneth, and scourgeth every son whom he receiveth. 7 If ye endure chastening, God dealeth with you as with sons; for what son is he whom the father chasteneth not? 8 But if ye be without chastisement, whereof all are partakers, then are ye bastards, and not sons. 9 Furthermore we have had fathers of our flesh which corrected us, and we gave them reverence: shall we not much rather be in subjection unto the Father of spirits, and live? 10 For they verily for a few days chastened us after their own pleasure; but he for our profit, that we might be partakers of his holiness. 11 Now no chastening for the present seemeth to be joyous, but grievous: nevertheless afterward it yieldeth the peaceable fruit of righteousness unto them which are exercised thereby.*

17. As God the Father works to secure the salvation of a soul, the Son works as well.

18. The believer is secure because of the promises Jesus Christ has made.

- *John 5:24 Verily, verily, I say unto you, He that heareth my word, and believeth on him that sent me, hath everlasting life, and shall not come into condemnation; but is passed from death unto life.*

- *John 6:37 All that the Father giveth me shall come to me; and him that cometh to me I will in no wise cast out.*

- *John 10:27-28 My sheep hear my voice, and I know them, and they follow me: 28 And I give unto them eternal life; and they shall never perish, neither shall any man pluck them out of my hand.*

19. The believer is secure because of the prayer of Christ for His own.

- *John 17:9 I pray for them: I pray not for the world, but for them which thou hast given me; for they are thine. 10 And all mine are thine, and thine are mine; and I am glorified in them. 11 And now I am no more in the world, but these are in the world, and I come to thee. Holy Father, keep through thine own name those whom thou hast given me, that they may be one, as we are. 12 While I was with them in the world, I kept them in thy name: those that thou gavest me I have kept, and none of them is lost, but the son of perdition; that the scripture might be fulfilled.*

- *John 17:15 I pray not that thou shouldest take them out of the world, but that thou shouldest keep them from the evil.*

- *John 17:20 Neither pray I for these alone, but for them also which shall believe on me through their word.*

20. The believer is secure because of the death Jesus died.

- *Isaiah 53:5 But he was wounded for our transgressions, he was bruised for our iniquities: the chastisement of our peace was upon him; and with his stripes we are healed. 11 He shall see of the travail of his soul, and shall be satisfied: by his knowledge shall my righteous servant justify many; for he shall bear their iniquities.*

- *Matthew 26:28 For this is my blood of the new testament, which is shed for many for the remission of sins.*

- *John 19:30 When Jesus therefore had received the vinegar, he said, It is finished: and he bowed his head, and gave up the ghost.*

In the death of Christ the law of double jeopardy is brought into view. This law states that a man cannot be tried or punished twice for the same crime. Through His death Christ was punished for the sins of the elect. By accepting him as Savior a sinner receives the forgiveness that comes when a sin debt is paid. However, if a person must still eventually pay for their own sin in hell because there was a fall from grace prior to death then the righteous Judge of the universe becomes guilty of breaking the law of double jeopardy.

21. The believer is secure because of the resurrection of Christ.

- *Romans 6:3 Know ye not, that so many of us as were baptized into Jesus Christ were baptized into his death? 4 Therefore we are buried with him by baptism into death: that like as Christ was raised up from the dead by the glory of the Father, even so we also should walk in newness of life. 5 For if we have been planted together in the likeness of his death, we shall be also in the likeness of his resurrection: 6 Knowing this, that our old man is crucified with him, that the body of sin might be destroyed, that henceforth we should not serve sin. 7 For he that is dead is freed from sin. 8 Now if we be dead with Christ, we believe that we shall also live with him: 9 Knowing that Christ being raised from the dead dieth no more; death hath no more dominion over him. 10 For in that he died, he died unto sin once: but in that he liveth, he liveth unto God.*

- *Colossians 2:12 Buried with him in baptism, wherein also ye are risen with him through the faith of the operation of God, who hath raised him from the dead. 13 And you, being dead in your sins and the uncircumcision of your flesh, hath he quickened together with him, having forgiven you all trespasses; 14 Blotting out the handwriting of ordinances that was against us, which was contrary to us, and took it out of the way, nailing it to his cross; 15 And having spoiled principalities and powers, he made a shew of them openly, triumphing over them in it.*

22. The believer is secure because of the present ministry of the Lord Jesus Christ on behalf of His own.

❖ Christ serves as an *advocate* [defense attorney] in heaven on behalf of those who are to be the heirs of salvation.

- *Romans 8:34 Who is he that condemneth? It is Christ that died, yea rather, that is risen again, who is even at the right hand of God, who also maketh intercession for us.*

- *Hebrews 9:24 For Christ is not entered into the holy places made with hands, which are the figures of the true; but into heaven itself, now to appear in the presence of God for us.*

- *1 John 2:1 My little children, these things write I unto you, that ye sin not. And if any man sin, we have an advocate with the Father, Jesus Christ the righteous.*

❖ Christ serves as a great *intercessor* in heaven for His own.

- *John 17 These words spake Jesus, and lifted up his eyes to heaven, and said, Father, the hour is come; glorify thy Son, that thy Son also may glorify thee: 2 As thou hast given him power over all flesh, that he should give eternal life to as many as thou hast given him. 3 And this is life eternal, that they might know thee the only true God, and Jesus Christ, whom thou hast sent. 4 I have glorified thee on the earth: I have finished the work which thou gavest me to do. 5 And now, O Father, glorify thou me with thine own self with the glory which I had with thee before the world was. 6 I have manifested thy name unto the men which thou gavest me out of the world: thine they were, and thou gavest them me; and they have kept thy word. 7 Now they have known that all things whatsoever thou hast given me are of thee. 8 For I have given unto them the words which thou gavest me; and they have received them, and have known surely that I came out from thee, and they have believed that thou didst send me. 9 I pray for them: I pray not for the world, but for them which thou hast given me; for they are thine. 10 And all mine are thine, and thine are mine; and I am glorified in them. 11 And now I am no more in the world, but these are in the world, and I come to thee. Holy Father, keep through thine own name those whom thou hast given me, that they may be one, as we are. 12 While I was with them in the world, I kept them in thy name: those that thou gavest me I have kept, and none of them is lost, but the son of perdition; that the scripture might be fulfilled. 13 And now come I to thee; and these things I speak in the world, that they might have my joy fulfilled in themselves. 14 I have given them thy word; and the world hath hated them, because they are not of the world, even as I am not of the world. 15 I pray not that thou shouldest take them out of the world, but that thou shouldest keep them from the evil. 16 They are not of the world, even as I am not of the world. 17 Sanctify them through thy truth: thy word is truth. 18 As thou hast sent me into the world, even so have I also sent them into the world. 19 And for their sakes I sanctify myself, that they also might be sanctified through the truth. 20 Neither pray I for these alone, but for them also which shall believe on me through their word; 21 That they all may be one; as thou, Father, art in me, and I in thee, that they also may be one in us: that the world may believe that thou hast sent me. 22 And the glory which thou gavest me I have given them; that they may be one, even as we are one: 23 I in them, and thou in me, that they may be made perfect in one; and that the world may know that thou hast sent me, and hast loved them, as thou hast loved me. 24 Father, I will that they also, whom thou hast given me, be with me where I am; that they may behold my glory, which thou hast given me: for thou lovedst me before the foundation of the world. 25 O righteous Father, the world hath not known thee: but I have known thee, and these have known that thou hast sent me. 26 And I have declared unto them thy name, and will declare it: that the love wherewith thou hast loved me may be in them, and I in them.*

- *Romans 8:34 Who is he that condemneth? It is Christ that died, yea rather, that is risen again, who is even at the right hand of God, who also maketh intercession for us.*

- *Hebrews 7:23 And they truly were many priests, because they were not suffered to continue by reason of death: 24 But this man, because he continueth ever, hath an unchangeable priesthood. 25 Wherefore he is able also to save them to the uttermost that come unto God by him, seeing he ever liveth to make intercession for them.*

   "For if, when we were enemies, we were reconciled to God by the death of his Son, much more, being reconciled, we shall be saved by his life."

The apostle Paul presents a most glorious truth. As Jesus Christ died to save sinners, so He will live to secure their salvation intact. Because of this ongoing redemption process Christ becomes the author of *eternal* salvation.

- *Hebrews 5:9 And being made perfect, he became the author of eternal salvation unto all them that obey him.*

23. In harmony with God the Father and God the Son, God the Holy Spirit works to secure the salvation of the believer.

24. The Holy Spirit is the agent of regeneration. It is the Holy Spirit who imparts new life into those who are born again. The believer has no confidence in the flesh to produce or to sustain life. His confidence is in the Holy Spirit.

- *John 3:3 Jesus answered and said unto him, Verily, verily, I say unto thee, Except a man be born again, he cannot see the kingdom of God. 4 Nicodemus saith unto him, How can a man be born when he is old? Can he enter the second time into his mother's womb, and be born? 5 Jesus answered, Verily, verily, I say unto thee, Except a man be born of water and of the Spirit, he cannot enter into the kingdom of God. 6 That which is born of the flesh is flesh; and that which is born of the Spirit is spirit. 7 Marvel not that I said unto thee, Ye must be born again.*

- *Titus 3:5 Not by works of righteousness which we have done, but according to his mercy he saved us, by the washing of regeneration, and renewing of the Holy Ghost.*

- *James 1:18 Of his own will begat he us with the word of truth, that we should be a kind of firstfruits of his creatures.*

- *1 Peter 1:23 Being born again, not of corruptible seed, but of incorruptible, by the word of God, which liveth and abideth for ever.*

21. When the Holy Spirit regenerates the soul there is a new nature that has an inclination to do what God wants done.

22. The assurance and security of the believer is cemented in a spiritual baptism into the body of Christ. So identified is the believer with the person and work of Christ that He becomes, in mystical marital language, part of the body of Christ, *"bone of His bone and flesh of His flesh."*

- *Romans 6:3 Know ye not, that so many of us as were baptized into Jesus Christ were baptized into his death? 4 Therefore we are buried with him by baptism into death: that like as Christ was raised up from the dead by the glory of the Father, even so we also should walk in newness of life.*

- *1 Corinthians 12:13 For by one Spirit are we all baptized into one body, whether we be Jews or Gentiles, whether we be bond or free; and have been all made to drink into one Spirit.*

- *Galatians 3:27 For as many of you as have been baptized into Christ have put on Christ.*

- *Ephesians 4:4-5 There is one body, and one Spirit, even as ye are called in one hope of your calling; One Lord, one faith, one baptism.*

- *Colossians 2:12 Buried with him in baptism, wherein also ye are risen with him through the faith of the operation of God, who hath raised him from the dead.*

23. To make certain the believer is secure in salvation for time and eternity the Holy Spirit indwells the soul. Many passages teach the present indwelling ministry of the Holy Spirit in the life of the Christian.

    - *John 7:37 In the last day, that great day of the feast, Jesus stood and cried, saying, If any man thirst, let him come unto me, and drink. 38 He that believeth on me, as the scripture hath said, out of his belly shall flow rivers of living water. 39 (But this spake he of the Spirit, which they that believe on him should receive: for the Holy Ghost was not yet given; because that Jesus was not yet glorified.)*

    - *John 14:16 And I will pray the Father, and he shall give you another Comforter, that he may abide with you for ever.*

    - *Romans 8:9 But ye are not in the flesh, but in the Spirit, if so be that the Spirit of God dwell in you. Now if any man have not the Spirit of Christ, he is none of his.*

    - *1 Corinthians 2:12 Now we have received, not the spirit of the world, but the spirit which is of God; that we might know the things that are freely given to us of God.*

    - *1 Corinthians 3:16 Know ye not that ye are the temple of God, and that the Spirit of God dwelleth in you?*

    - *1 Corinthians 6:19 What? Know ye not that your body is the temple of the Holy Ghost which is in you, which ye have of God, and ye are not your own?*

    - *1 John 3:24 And he that keepeth his commandments dwelleth in him, and he in him. And hereby we know that he abideth in us, by the Spirit which he hath given us.*

24. To make certain the believer is secure in salvation for time and eternity the Holy Spirit pledges Himself and seals the believer until the day of redemption. The day of redemption refers to the Second Coming of Christ as per Acts 1:11 and Hebrews 9:28.

    - *Ephesians 1:13 In whom ye also trusted, after that ye heard the word of truth, the gospel of your salvation: in whom also after that ye believed, ye were sealed with that holy Spirit of promise, 14 Which is the earnest [pledge] of our inheritance until the redemption of the purchased possession, unto the praise of his glory.*

    - *2 Corinthians 1:22 Who hath also sealed us, and given the earnest of the Spirit in our hearts.*

    - *2 Corinthians 5:5 Now he that hath wrought us for the selfsame thing is God, who also hath given unto us the earnest of the Spirit.*

    - *Ephesians 4:30 And grieve not the Holy Spirit of God, whereby ye are sealed unto the day of redemption.*

- *Acts 1:11 Which also said, Ye men of Galilee, why stand ye gazing up into heaven? This same Jesus, which is taken up from you into heaven, shall so come in like manner as ye have seen him go into heaven.*

- *Hebrews 9:28 So Christ was once offered to bear the sins of many; and unto them that look for him shall he appear the second time without sin unto salvation.*

25. To make certain the believer is secure in salvation for time and eternity the Holy Spirit strengthens the believer.

- *Ephesians 3:16 That he would grant you, according to the riches of his glory, to be strengthened with might by his Spirit in the inner man;*

26. To make certain the believer is secure in salvation for time and eternity the Holy Spirit prays for the believer.

- *Romans 8:26 Likewise the Spirit also helpeth our infirmities: for we know not what we should pray for as we ought: but the Spirit itself maketh intercession for us with groanings which cannot be uttered.*

32 Times the Term "Beloved" is Used

- *Song of Solomon 1:14 My beloved is unto me as a cluster of camphire…*

- *Song of Solomon 1:16 Behold, thou art fair, my beloved, yea, pleasant….*

- *Song of Solomon 2:3 As the apple tree among the trees of the wood, so is my beloved among the sons…*

- *Song of Solomon 2:8 The voice of my beloved! Behold, he cometh leaping upon the mountains, skipping upon the hills.*

- *Song of Solomon 2:9 My beloved is like a roe or a young hart…..*

- *Song of Solomon 2:10 My beloved spake, and said unto me, Rise up, my love….*

- *Song of Solomon 2:16 My beloved is mine, and I am his…*

- *Song of Solomon 2:17 …turn, my beloved, and be thou like a roe or a young hart upon the mountains of Bether.*

- *Song of Solomon 4:16 …Let my beloved come into his garden, and eat his pleasant fruits.*

- *Song of Solomon 5:1 …eat, O friends; drink, yea, drink abundantly, O beloved.*

- *Song of Solomon 5:2 I sleep, but my heart waketh: it is the voice of my beloved…*

- *Song of Solomon 5:4 My beloved put in his hand by the hole of the door, and my bowels [emotions] were moved for him.*

- *Song of Solomon 5:5 I rose up to open to my beloved….*

- *Song of Solomon 5:6 I opened to my beloved; but my beloved had withdrawn himself, and was gone: my soul failed when he spake: I sought him, but I could not find him…*

- *Song of Solomon 5:8 … if ye find my beloved, that ye tell him, that I am sick of love.*

- *Song of Solomon 5:9 What is thy beloved more than another beloved…*

- *Song of Solomon 5:10 My beloved is white and ruddy, the chiefest among ten thousand.*

- *Song of Solomon 5:16 …This is my beloved, and this is my friend, O daughters of Jerusalem.*

- *Song of Solomon 6:1 Whither is thy beloved gone….*

- *Song of Solomon 6:2 My beloved is gone down into his garden, to the beds of spices…*

- *Song of Solomon 6:3 I am my beloved's, and my beloved is mine….*

- *Song of Solomon 7:9 And the roof of thy mouth like the best wine for my beloved, that goeth down sweetly…*

- *Song of Solomon 7:11 Come, my beloved, let us go forth into the field…..*

- *Song of Solomon 7:13 The mandrakes give a smell…which I have laid up for thee, O my beloved.*

- *Song of Solomon 8:5 Who is this that cometh up from the wilderness, leaning upon her beloved?*

- *Song of Solomon 8:14 Make haste, my beloved, and be thou like to a roe or to a young hart upon the mountains of spices.*

SONG OF SOLOMON 3

The Shulamite Maiden Dreams a Dream

1 By night on my bed I sought him whom my soul loveth: I sought him, but I found him not.

3:1 I found him not. For some reason the Shulamite maiden had a sense of losing the sweet fellowship of her beloved. Spiritually, this sense of loss is not unique. David once cried out, *"LORD, by thy favour thou hast made my mountain to stand strong: thou didst hide thy face, and I was troubled"* (Psa. 30:7).

"But flowers need night's cool sweetness,
The moonlight and the dew;
So Christ from one who loved Him,

> His presence oft withdrew."
>
> Rutherford
>
> Spiritual Causes for the Dark Night of the Soul
>
> - Grieving the Holy Spirit   Ephesians 4:30
> - Quenching the Holy Spirit   1 Thessalonians 5:19
> - Lying to the Holy Spirit   Acts 5:3
> - Resisting the Holy Spirit   Acts 7:51
> - Blaspheming the Holy Spirit   Matthew 12:31

2 I will rise now, and go about the city in the streets, and in the broad ways I will seek him whom my soul loveth: I sought him, but I found him not.

> 3:2 **I will rise now.** Realizing her loss the Shulamite maiden makes every effort to restore broken fellowship. In like manner the Christian must make every effort to restore fellowship with the Lord.
> ### Recovery of Spiritual Fellowship
>
> - Confession. *1 John 1:9 If we confess our sins, he is faithful and just to forgive us our sins, and to cleanse us from all unrighteousness.*
>
> - Putting away sin. *Hebrews 12:1 Wherefore seeing we also are compassed about with so great a cloud of witnesses, let us lay aside every weight, and the sin which doth so easily beset us, and let us run with patience the race that is set before us,*

> - Having the mind of Christ. Philippians 2:5 Let this mind be in you , which was also in Christ Jesus:
>
> - Walk in the light. 1 John 1:7 But if we walk in the light, as he is in the light, we have fellowship one with another, and the blood of Jesus Christ his Son cleanseth us from all sin.
>
> - Love not the world. *1 John 2:15 Love not the world, neither the things that are in the world. If any man love the world, the love of the Father is not in him.*

3 The watchmen that go about the city found me: *to whom I said*, Saw ye him whom my soul loveth?

> 3:1 **saw ye him.** To the watchman the question might have appeared incoherent. To the Shulamite woman there was only one person whom who heart was fixed on. The Christian must have but One person and one passion. *Matthew 6:33 But seek ye first the kingdom of God, and his righteousness; and all these things shall be added unto you.*

4 *It was* but a little that I passed from them, but I found him whom my soul loveth: I held him, and would not let him go, until I had brought him into my mother's house, and into the chamber of her that conceived me.

3:4 I found him. As the Shulamite maiden found her beloved so the heart that seeks after the Lord shall find Him. *Jeremiah 29:13 And ye shall seek me, and find me, when ye shall search for me with all your heart.*

"Safe in the arms of Jesus,
safe on His gentle breast,
There by His love o'ershaded,
sweetly my soul shall rest.

Hark! 'Tis the voice of angels,
borne in a song to me.
Over the fields of glory,
over the jasper sea.

Safe in the arms of Jesus,
safe on His gentle breast
There by His love o'ershaded,
Sweetly my soul shall rest.

Safe in the arms of Jesus,
safe from corroding care,
Safe from the world's temptations,
sin cannot harm me there.

Free from the blight of sorrow,
free from my doubts and fears;
Only a few more trials,
only a few more tears!

Jesus, my heart's dear Refuge,
Jesus has died for me;
Firm on the Rock of Ages,
ever my trust shall be.

Here let me wait with patience,
wait till the night is over;
Wait till I see the morning
break on the golden shore".

The Story Behind the Song

On April 30, 1868, Dr. W. H. Doane came into my house and said, *"I have exactly forty minutes before my train leaves for Cincinnati. Here is a melody. Can you write words for it?"* I replied that I would see what I could do. Then followed a space of twenty minutes during which I was wholly unconscious of all else except the work I was doing. At the end of that time I recited the words to *"Safe in the Arms of Jesus."* Mr. Doane copied them, and had time to catch his train.

5 I charge you, O ye daughters of Jerusalem, by the roes, and by the hinds of the field, that ye stir not up, nor awake *my* love, till he please.

The Daughters of Jerusalem Describe a Marriage Procession with Solomon Arrayed in all his Glory

6 Who *is* this that cometh out of the wilderness like pillars of smoke [incense], perfumed with myrrh and frankincense, with all powders of the merchant?

3:6 Who is this. The Shulamite maiden has waited long for her expected bridegroom to return and now the grand day has arrived. People in the country side join in the excitement and wonder as they say, *"Who is this that cometh?"* Attention is focused upon the son of David.

7 Behold his bed, which *is* Solomon's; threescore [60] valiant men [as bodyguards] *are* about it, of the valiant of Israel.

3:7 behold. The royal entourage is recognized. Sixty strong warriors guard the king as the sovereign moves among the shepherds and vinedressers.

8 They all hold swords, *being* expert in war: every man *hath* his sword upon his thigh because of fear in the night.

3:8 hold swords. No one will be allowed to hurt the king as he moves among the masses. This is his crowning hour and it is most glorious. In like manner no one will ever again hurt Jesus Christ. One day He too will come to claim His bride in a more visible manner. It will be a glorious coming.

> "He is coming as the Bridegroom,
> Coming to unfold at last
> The great secret of His purpose,
> Mystery of ages past;
> And the bride, to her is granted,
> In His beauty now to shine,
> As in rapture she exclaimeth,
> 'I am His, and He is mine!'
> Oh, what joy that marriage union,
> Mystery of love divine;
> Sweet to sing in all its fullness,
> 'I am His, and He is mine!'"

Biblical Marriages setting forth in Typology the Church and Christ

- Adam and Eve

- Isaac and Rebecca
- Jacob and Rachel
- Joseph and his Gentile wife
- Boaz and Ruth
- Every Christian man who marries a Christian woman

Ephesians 5:25 Husbands, love your wives, even as Christ also loved the church, and gave himself for it; 26 That he might sanctify and cleanse it with the washing of water by the word, 27 That he might present it to himself a glorious church, not having spot, or wrinkle, or any such thing; but that it should be holy and without blemish.

9 King Solomon made himself a chariot [a bed] of the wood of Lebanon.

3:9 Lebanon (le-ba'-na; white), refers to a mountain range of Syria. The forests of the area provided a source of refuge (Jer. 22:23).

10 He made the pillars thereof of silver, the bottom thereof of gold, the covering of it of purple, the midst thereof being paved *with* love, for the daughters of Jerusalem.

The Shulamite Maiden

11 Go forth, O ye daughters of Zion, and behold king Solomon with the crown wherewith his mother crowned him in the day of his espousals, and in the day of the gladness of his heart.

3:11 Zion (zi'-un; fortification), refers to Jerusalem, the city of David and the city of God.

SONG OF SOLOMON 4

Solomon

1 Behold, thou *art* fair, my love; behold, thou *art* fair; thou hast doves' eyes within thy locks [curls of hair]: thy hair is as a flock of goats, that appear from mount Gilead.

4:1 thou art fair. Four times in this chapter Solomon declares the Shulamite maiden is fair though she views herself as being *"black as the tents of Kedar"*. Spiritually, how kind is Christ to look at the church as altogether lovely and something to be desired.

"Amazing grace, how sweet the sound,
That saved a wretch like me."

4:1 dove's eyes. Physically the dove has excellent sight. It can see clearly. Spiritually that is significant for the dove was ceremonially a clean bird. It was a bird that could be offered on an altar as it typified the Holy Spirit who came like a dove upon Christ and who comes into every heart to guide clearly the believer along the path that should be traveled in the journey of grace.

4:1 thy hair. The Syrian goat enjoys long silken hair. Solomon looked at the loveliness of the Shulamite maiden and said, *"Your hair is long and silken and I am reminded of it when I look upon the beauty of the scene of a flock of goats on the mountain side."* In the *Bible,* hair represents the glory of a woman which is why she is not to cut and cast away too quickly her beauty and glory.

The story is told in the *New Testament* of a woman who once knelt before Jesus in tears and wiped His feet with that which represented her glory and beauty (John 11:2).

4:1 Gilead (ghil'-e-ad; rugged), refers to a mountain region east of the Jordan River 3,000 feet above sea level.

2 Thy teeth are like a flock *of sheep that are even* shorn, which came up from the washing; whereof every one bear twins, and none is barren among them.

4:2 thy teeth. A nice set of pearly white teeth are lovely. They answer to the twins in their cleanliness and sparkling beauty. Spiritual teeth are also vital for the Christian must *"eat"* of Christ and be able to *"digest"* the Word of God. *Jeremiah 15:16 Thy words were found, and I did eat them; and thy word was unto me the joy and rejoicing of mine heart: for I am called by thy name, O LORD God of hosts.*

3 Thy lips *are* like a thread of scarlet, and thy speech is comely: thy temples *are* like a piece of a pomegranate within thy locks.

4:3 thy lips. Here are red lips of natural health as there should be red lips of natural spiritual health.

4:3 thy speech is comely. The speech is comely or pleasing because the language is about Christ. *Malachi 3:16 Then they that feared the LORD spake often one to another: and the LORD hearkened, and heard it, and a book of remembrance was written before him for them that feared the LORD, and that thought upon his name.* Many commandments come to guard the speech. *Colossians 4:6 Let your speech be alway with grace, seasoned with salt, that ye may know how ye ought to answer every man.*

4:3 thy temples. The temples speak of the place of thought and so the Church must think often about Christ as the Shulamite maiden thought much about Solomon and he of her. *Psalms 77:12 I will meditate also of all thy work, and talk of thy doings.*

4 Thy neck *is* like the tower of David builded for an armoury, whereon there hang a thousand bucklers, all shields of mighty men.

4:4 thy neck is like the tower of David. The tower of David was a place of defense. It was well fortified. The character of a godly woman is her tower of defense. She can say no to temptation. She can say yes to righteousness. She holds her head high with grace and courage. The church is called upon to be *"strong in the Lord, and in the power of His might" (Eph. 6:10).* The believer has no strength in and of himself. His hope and strength is in the Lord.

5 Thy two breasts *are* like two young roes that are twins, which feed among the lilies.

4:5 thy two breasts. Solomon speaks of that which indicates the place of tender affection and intimate love. The heart of the Shulamite maiden belongs to him and he knows it. Well may the church sing of the personal value of Christ.

> I want no better Friend;
> I trust Him now,
> I'll trust Him when life's fleeting days shall end.
>
> Beautiful life with such a Friend,
> beautiful life that has no end;
> Eternal life, eternal joy,
> He's my Friend."
>
> Will L. Thompson, 1904

6 Until the day break, and the shadows flee away, I will get me to the mountain of myrrh, and to the hill of frankincense.

> 4:6 myrrh refers to an aromatic resin that was highly valued. The sap is collected by making a cut in the main trunk.
>
> 4:6 frankincense refers to a fragrant bitter tasting gum resin that was extracted from various varieties of the balsam tree in east Africa and in south Arabia.

7 Thou *art* all fair, my love; there is no spot in thee.

> 4:1-7
>
> Seven Perfect Parts of the
> Maiden's Body
>
> - Eyes
> - Hair
> - Teeth
> - Lips
> - Temples
> - Neck
> - Breasts

8 Come with me from Lebanon, *my* spouse [bride], with me from Lebanon: look from the top of Amana, from the top of Shenir and Hermon, from the lions' dens, from the mountains of the leopards.

> 4:8 come with me. Here is a royal summons to fellowship. The church has received a royal invitation from Christ to fellowship with Him.
>
> "Jesus has a table spread
> Where the saints of God are fed,
> He invites His chosen people,
> "Come and dine";
> With His manna He doth feed
> And supplies our every need:
> O 'tis sweet to sup with Jesus all the time!

"Come and dine," the Master calleth,
"Come and dine";
You may feast at Jesus' table
all the time;

He Who fed the multitude,
turned the water into wine,
To the hungry calleth now,
"Come and dine."

The disciples came to land,
Thus obeying Christ's command,
For the Master called unto them, "Come and dine";
There they found their heart's desire,
Bread and fish upon the fire;
Thus He satisfies the hungry every time.

Soon the Lamb will take His bride
To be ever at His side,
All the host of Heaven
will assembled be;
O 'twill be a glorious sight,
All the saints in spotless white;
And with Jesus they will feast eternally."

Charles B. Widmeyer, 1906

4:8 Lebanon (le-ba'-na; white), refers to a mountain range of Syria. The cedars of Lebanon symbolized pride (Psa. 29:5-6; Isa. 2:13; 10:34).

4:8 Amana (am-a'-nah; fixed, firmness; a treaty, covenant), refers to the northern mountain ridge of Antilibanus (Song. of Song 4:8). From here the water of Abana flows.

4:8 Shenir (she'-nur; coat of mail), Senir, refers to the mountain between Amanah and Hermon, at the northeast of Jordan (Deut. 3:9; Ezek. 27:5).

4:8 Hermon, Mt. (her'-mon; lofty), has three peaks. The summons of the mountain is covered with snow all year round. The water for the Jordan River has its source on Mt. Hermon.

9 Thou hast ravished [taken away] my heart, my sister, *my* spouse [bride]; thou hast ravished my heart with one of thine eyes, with one chain of thy neck.

4:9 Thou hast ravished my heart. Solomon was captivated by the Shulamite maiden. In matchless grace the attitude of Christ towards the church is one of absolute captivation. Why this
is so is beyond understanding this side of eternity but it is a grand and glorious truth to consider.

"Wondrous it seemeth to me
Jesus so gracious should be,
Mercy revealing, comforting, healing,
Blessing a sinner like me.

Is it not wonderful, is it not wonderful
Jesus so gracious should be?
Yes, it is wonderful, strange
and so wonderful
That He should pardon
and save even me!"

Elisha A. Hoffman, 1899

4:9 my sister. A term of affection and endearment.

10 How fair is thy love, my sister, *my* spouse! How much better is thy love than wine! And the smell [fragrance] of thine ointments [perfume] than all spices!

4:10 the smell. The Shulamite maiden had a sweet smell about her personage that was pleasing to Solomon. So every Christian should be a sweet smelling savor unto Christ (Phil. 4:18) and will be when they are occupied with the person of Christ.

11 Thy lips, O *my* spouse, drop *as* the honeycomb: honey and milk *are* under thy tongue; and the smell of thy garments *is* like the smell of Lebanon.

12 A garden inclosed [fenced in] *is* my sister, *my* spouse; a spring shut up, a fountain sealed.

4:12 a garden inclosed. As the Shulamite maiden was alone with Solomon so the Christian is to be alone with Christ for the church is likened to a garden.

- *Jeremiah 31:12 Therefore they shall come and sing in the height of Zion, and shall flow together to the goodness of the LORD, for wheat, and for wine, and for oil, and for the young of the flock and of the herd: and their soul shall be as a watered garden; and they shall not sorrow any more at all.*

The idea of separation is part of the garden concept. The Christian is to live a holy and separated life from the world, the flesh, and the devil.

- *Psalms 4:3 But know that the LORD hath set apart him that is godly for himself: the LORD will hear when I call unto him.*

The concept of being able to better protect the contents of a garden is found in its being enclosed. Intimacy, separation, and holiness, these are the characteristics of a spiritual garden of divine delight.

4:12 a spring shut up. Because pure water is precious in the Middle East, when a spring was discovered it was walled about, covered and locked. The owner would guard access to the water supply while keeping the pool from pollution and waste. In matchless grace God has given to every believer living waters to drink. This living water is designed to water the spiritual garden of divine delight to bring forth spiritual fruit: *"the fruit of the Spirit is love, joy, peace, longsuffering, gentleness, goodness, faith, 23Meekness, temperance: against such there is no law" (Galatians 5:22-23).*

13 Thy plants *are* an orchard of pomegranates, with pleasant fruits; camphire, with spikenard,

14 Spikenard and saffron; calamus and cinnamon, with all trees of frankincense; myrrh and aloes, with all the chief spices:

4:14 plants. The purpose of a garden is not only to look lovely but to produce. The purpose of the church is not just to appear lovely but to produce spiritual fruit for the Lord.

- *Philippians 1:9 And this I pray, that your love may abound yet more and more in knowledge and in all judgment; 10 That ye may approve things that are excellent; that ye may be sincere and without offence till the day of Christ; 11 Being filled with the fruits of righteousness, which are by Jesus Christ, unto the glory and praise of God.*

4:14 spikenard refers to a rose red fragrant ointment made from the dried roots of a plant growing in the mountains of northern India.

4:14 saffron, a sweet smelling plant with purplish flowers and orange stigmas. The plant was used for a dye, seasoning, and medicine.

4:14 calamus (cal'-a-mus), refers to a sweet fragrant reed plant. It was one of the substances Moses used to make the oil used for anointing (Ex. 30:23). The plant was used for medicinal purposes of gastric complaints.

4:14 cinnamon. The cinnamon tree was not found in Palestine during biblical days. The sweet smelling bark was highly prized as it was brought from China to Judea by the Phoenicians and the Arabs in caravans traveling through Persia.

4:14 frankincense refers to a fragrant bitter tasting gum resin that was extracted from various varieties of the balsam tree in east Africa and in south Arabia.

4:14 myrrh refers to an aromatic resin that was highly valued. The resin sap has a clear, oily consistency and is white or yellowish in color.

4:14 aloes refers to a plant which produced oil which provided valued perfume.

4:14 spice may refer to the mastic tree which is an evergreen. This small deciduous shrub has composite leafs which consists of eight smaller leaves. These contain fragrant volatile oils which are emitted when the leaves are crushed. The trunk and thicker branches contain resin, which is released when the bark is cut. It is a pale color, or sometimes greenish, and has a pleasant odor and taste. Oil is pressed from the small, round brownish-black root which was used for cooking and in loaves. The resin and oil of the mastic tree was used for embalming.

15 A fountain of gardens, a well of living waters, and streams from Lebanon.

4:15 streams from Lebanon. Lebanon contains the backbone mountain range of Palestine. To the north is Mt. Hermon with the peak covered with snow. The streams from Lebanon flow into the ground creating springs to rise in vales and dells. These streams become living water to thirsty travelers and speak of the Holy Spirit.

Jesus said, "...*If any man thirst, let him come unto me, and drink. 38 He that believeth on me, as the scripture hath said, out of his belly shall flow rivers of living water. 39 (But this spake he of the Spirit, which they that believe on him should receive: for the Holy Ghost was not yet given; because that Jesus was not yet glorified.)" (John 7:37-39).*

The Spirit of God descends from above and enters into the soul that is born again to provide living water springing up unto everlasting life. The heart of a Christian is refreshed to know it is loved and there is hope beyond the grave because sins are forgiven.

The Shulamite Maiden

16 Awake, O north wind; and come, thou south; blow upon my garden, *that* the spices thereof may flow out. Let my beloved come into his garden, and eat his pleasant fruits.

4:16 awake. The Shulamite maiden responds to the language of love and desires the north wind to blow that she might be at her best for her beloved. She wants to be like him and for him. So the church desires to be for Christ and like Him.

"O to be like Thee! Blessed Redeemer,
This is my constant longing and prayer;
Gladly I'll forfeit all of earth's treasures,
Jesus, Thy perfect likeness to wear.

O to be like Thee! O to be like Thee,
Blessèd Redeemer, pure as Thou art;
Come in Thy sweetness,
Come in Thy fullness;
Stamp Thine own image
Deep on my heart.

O to be like Thee! Full of compassion,
Loving, forgiving, tender and kind,
Helping the helpless,
Cheering the fainting,
Seeking the wandering sinner to find.

O to be like Thee! Lowly in spirit,
Holy and harmless, patient and brave;
Meekly enduring cruel reproaches,
Willing to suffer others to save.

O to be like Thee! Lord, I am coming
Now to receive anointing divine;
All that I am and have I am bringing,
Lord, from this moment
All shall be Thine.

O to be like Thee! While I am pleading,
Pour out Thy Spirit, fill with Thy love;
Make me a temple
Meet for Thy dwelling,
Fit me for life and Heaven above".

Thomas O. Chisholm, 1897

With the blowing of the north wind the fruit was more perfect. In like manner with adversity the Christian is perfected. One day Charles Spurgeon was visiting a farmer and noticed the words *"God is love"* painted on his weathervane. *"Do you mean that God's love is as changeable as the wind?"* asked Mr. Spurgeon. *"No,"* replied the farmer. *"I mean that whichever way the wind blows God is love."* As the northern winds are needed so are the southern winds. The cold is needed to bring out the taste in apples and the summer weather is needed for them to ripe. God knows how to bring forth spiritual fruit as well with a mixture of harshness and warmth. The end result will be sweet fellowship. *"Let my beloved come into his garden, and eat his pleasant fruits."*

4:14 cinnamon. The cinnamon tree was not found in Palestine during biblical days. The sweet smelling bark was highly prized as it was brought from China to Judea by the Phoenicians and the Arabs in caravans traveling through Persia.

Various books of the *Bible* were read annually at different feasts.

• Passover	Song of Solomon
• Pentecost	Ruth
• On the 9th of Ab (August)	Lamentations
• Feast of Tabernacles	Ecclesiastes
• Purim	Esther

SONG OF SOLOMON 5

Solomon

1 I am come into my garden, my sister, *my* spouse: I have gathered my myrrh with my spice; I have eaten my honeycomb with my honey; I have drunk my wine with my milk: eat,

5:1 I am come. In the journey in grace there are sweet times of fellowship with the Lord. Communion is precious and the soul draws close to the heart of God.

> "There is a place of quiet rest,
> Near to the heart of God.
> A place where sin cannot molest,
> Near to the heart of God.
>
> O Jesus, blest Redeemer,
> Sent from the heart of God,
> Hold us who wait before Thee
> Near to the heart of God.
>
> There is a place of comfort sweet,
> Near to the heart of God.
> A place where we our Savior meet,
> Near to the heart of God.
>
> There is a place of full release,
> Near to the heart of God.
> A place where all is joy and peace,
> Near to the heart of God."
>
> Cleland B. McAfee, 1903

The Daughters of Jerusalem

O friends; drink, yea, drink abundantly, O beloved.

The Shulamite Maiden

2 I sleep, but my heart waketh: *it is* the voice of my beloved that knocketh, *saying,* Open to me, my sister, my love, my dove, my undefiled: for my head is filled with dew, *and* my locks with the drops of the night.

> 5:2 I sleep. As there are sweet times of communion in the journey of grace so there are times when that fellowship is interrupted. Often that period of disruption is soon after the enjoyment of closeness. Why this is so is a spiritual mystery but it does seem as if the world, the flesh and the devil unite to rob the Christian of joy. The Lord comes knocking on the door of the heart but Love is turned away. Oh the perverseness of the human heart! How willful is the soul! How full of unbelief!

3 I have put off my coat; how shall I put it on? I have washed my feet; how shall I defile them?

> 5:3 I have put off. One wicked excuse is piled on top of another as to why the heart will not do right. One rationale after another is given to do wrong. The soul whispers thoughts to itself thereby leading self into evil with small steps towards self absorption which is the essence of all sin. This self centeredness is rooted in unbelief.

- In essence the heart believes that God can be mocked and refuses to believe He will not be. The patience of God is abused.

- The heart believes there is no penalty for transgression of God's holy law because there is a time delay in which the grace of God and His mercy is not exhausted. Time is given to stand in self judgment and repent. Nevertheless, unbelief in a certain and fearful judgment is made manifest.

- The heart does not believe God will leave a soul to its own devises much like a parent will allow a willful child to vent.

4 My beloved put in his hand by the hole *of the door*, and my bowels [deepest emotions] were moved for him.

5 I rose up to open to my beloved; and my hands dropped *with* myrrh, and my fingers *with* sweet smelling myrrh, upon the handles of the lock.

5:5 my hands dropped. It was a custom when visiting to leave evidence of having called. The maiden knows her lover has been to see her. It was not a dream. But the problem was this: she had all time for herself and no time for him. It was not convenient.

6 I opened to my beloved; but my beloved had withdrawn himself, *and* was gone: my soul failed when he spake: I sought him, but I could not find him; I called him, but he gave me no answer.

5:6 had withdrawn.

- Sin causes the Lord to withdraw.
- Sin causes the Lord to go away.
- Sin causes the soul to not find the Lord for the will is dulled and the heart is heavy. Spiritual energy is drained.
- Sin causes the heart to call upon the Lord only to be discouraged at the sound of silence. "*He gave no answer.*"
- Sin brings the soul to despair.

"Where is the blessedness I knew
When first I saw the Lord?"

7 The watchmen that went about the city found me, they smote me, they wounded me; the keepers of the walls took away my veil from me.

5:7 they wounded me. The Shulamite maiden realizes how foolish she has been to turn away a time of fellowship with her lover. Now she goes to seek for him and finds herself the subject of suffering.

Spiritually, *"You will always have to suffer if you refuse obedience to the voice of Christ when He calls you"* (Dr. H. A. Ironside).

The Suffering in the Soul Due to Sin

- There is the affliction of a guilty conscience.
- There is the knowledge that precious time has been wasted instead of redeemed.
- There is the shame of secret sin.
- There are emotional scars such as the loss of self respect.
- There is self loathing and self berating for being so stupid, stubborn and self centered.
- There is the fact that distinguishing marks are lost. The Shulamite woman was wounded because she had lost her veil. With the loss of the veil came the loss of her power to protect herself. She was viewed as a low woman of character and treated as such. Oh Christian, do not lose you spiritual veil. Do not let sin remove your power.

8 I charge [command] you, O daughters of Jerusalem, if ye find my beloved, that ye tell him, that I *am* sick [faint] of love [with desire].

5: 8 sick of love. The Shulamite maiden appeals to the daughters of Jerusalem to help her be reconciled with her lover. Spiritually, an appeal must be made to find restoration to fellowship with the Savior.

How to be Restored to Spiritual Fellowship

- There must be repentance as deep and genuine as the transgression.
- Time must be redeemed.
- A search must be made for the face of God.
- All other matters in life must be set aside.
- Every means and every person must be used and appealed to in the process. King Jeroboam asked the man of God to pray for him and so must you and so must I (1 Kings 13:6).
- Praise and worship will move the heart of God and help restore spiritual fellowship.

The Daughters of Jerusalem

9 What is thy beloved more than *another* beloved, O thou fairest among women? What is thy beloved more than *another* beloved, that thou dost so charge us?

5:9 charge us. The Daughters of Jerusalem are left wondering how the Shulamite maiden came to need their help. Why has she allowed her communion with her lover to be interrupted? The same question can be asked spiritually. Why does the heart of the Christian allow sin to disrupt fellowship with the Lord? No answer for the *"why"* of sin is satisfactory. Because any sin is an irrational act it is almost impossible to give a rationale explanation for evil. Undergirding the mystery of sin is the will to power and the principle of personal pleasure. Despite the fact the pleasure does not last and there is shame and guilt on the other side of the moment the heart continues to do wrong and the horrible question is asked again, *"Why?"*

The Shulamite Maiden

10 My beloved is white and ruddy, the chiefest among ten thousand.

11 His head *is as* the most fine gold, his locks are bushy, and black as a raven.

12 His eyes *are as the eyes* of doves by the rivers of waters, washed with milk, and fitly set.

13 His cheeks *are* as a bed of spices, *as* sweet [fragrant] flowers: his lips *like* lilies, dropping sweet smelling myrrh.

14 His hands *are* as gold rings set with the beryl: his belly is as bright ivory overlaid *with* sapphires.

5:14 beryl (ber'-il), refers to a precious stone, probably golden or yellow in color.

15 His legs *are* as pillars of marble, set upon sockets of fine gold: his countenance is as Lebanon, excellent as the cedars.

5:15 Lebanon (le-ba'-na; white), refers to a mountain range of Syria. The area provided some of the best building material which was supplied to Egypt, Mesopotamia, and Palestine (1 Kings 5:6, 9, 14; 2 Chron. 2:8).

16 His mouth *is* most sweet: yea, he *is* altogether lovely. This *is* my beloved, and this *is* my friend, O daughters of Jerusalem.

5:10-16 My beloved. The mind used to rationalize sin must be re-employed to recognize God. As the Shulamite maiden praised her lover so the erring Christian must engage in spiritual worship and praise. The Shulamite maiden honored the kindness, graciousness, willingness to help, the strength and tenderness of her lover. So the Christian must praise the Lord for His tenderness, His long suffering, His willingness to help the unworthy, and his mercies which are renewed each day.

> "Great is Thy faithfulness,
> O God my Father;
> There is no shadow
> of turning with Thee;
>
> Thou changest not,
> Thy compassions, they fail not;
> As Thou hast been,
> Thou forever will be.
>
> Great is Thy faithfulness!
> Great is Thy faithfulness!

Morning by morning new mercies I see.
All I have needed
Thy hand hath provided;
Great is Thy faithfulness,
Lord, unto me!

Summer and winter
and springtime and harvest,
Sun, moon and stars
in their courses above
Join with all nature in manifold witness
To Thy great faithfulness,
mercy and love.

Pardon for sin
and a peace that endureth
Thine own dear presence to cheer
and to guide;

Strength for today
and bright hope for tomorrow,
Blessings all mine,
with ten thousand beside!"

Thomas O. Chisholm, 1923

SONG OF SOLOMON 6

The Daughters of Jerusalem

1 Whither is thy beloved gone, O thou fairest among women? Whither is thy beloved turned aside? That we may seek him with thee.

The Shulamite Maiden

2 My beloved is gone down into his garden, to the beds of spices, to feed in the gardens, and to gather lilies.

6:2 into his garden. The Shulamite maiden remembered where she last enjoyed communion with her lover and returned there. In like manner the Christian should return to his spiritual *"Bethel"* where he first met the Lord (Gen. 35:1).

3 I *am* my beloved's, and my beloved *is* mine: he feedeth among the lilies.

> 6:3 I am my beloved's. Here is the sweet reunion of two hearts as one. The Shulamite maiden has found her lover and all is once more right. When the heart of a Christian returns to Christ all is right and tender words of love can be exchanged once more.

Solomon

4 Thou *art* beautiful, O my love, as Tirzah, comely as Jerusalem, terrible as *an army* with banners.

> 6:4 Tirzah (tur'-zah; delight), was located 7 miles NE of Shechem. Tirzah was the capital of Israel until the days of Omri (1 Kings 14:17).

5 Turn away thine eyes from me, for they have overcome me: thy hair *is* as a flock of goats that appear from Gilead.

> 6:5 Gilead (ghil'-e-ad; rugged), refers to a mountain region E of the Jordan River extending from the Sea of Galilee to the upper end of the Dead Sea.

6 Thy teeth *are* as a flock of sheep which go up from the washing, whereof every one beareth twins, and *there is* not one barren among them.

7 As a piece of a pomegranate *are* thy temples within thy locks.

8 There are threescore [60] queens, and fourscore [80] concubines, and virgins without number.

> 6:8 threescore…fourscore. In time Solomon would embrace 700 queens and 300 concubines (1 Kings 11:3).

9 My dove, my undefiled [pure one] is but one; she *is* the *only* one of her mother, she *is* the choice one of her that bare her. The daughters saw her, and blessed her; yea, the queens and the concubines, and they praised her.
10 Who *is* she *that* looketh forth as the morning, fair as the moon, clear as the sun, and terrible as *an army* with banners?
11 I went down into the garden of nuts to see the fruits of the valley, *and* to see whether the vine flourished, *and* the pomegranates budded.
12 Or ever I was aware, my soul made me *like* the chariots of Amminadib.

> 6:12 Amminadib (am-min'-a-dib; my people is liberal), is another form of Amminadab. His chariots are mentioned as being swift (Song 6:12).

The Daughters of Jerusalem

13 Return, return, O Shulamite; return, return, that we may look upon thee.

6:13 Shulamite. The last wife of David was called the Shunamite (1 Kings 1:3). The benefactor of Elisha was called a Shunammite from Shunem (2 Kings 4:8, 12, 25, 36). Shunem was a town in Issachar (Josh. 1918; 1 Sam. 28:4).

Solomon

What will ye see in the Shulamite? As it were the company of two armies.

6:13 Shulamite, Shulammite (shu'-lam-ite; peaceful). The term is used for the young woman who loved the shepherd.

Doctrine of Women

The New Testament Teaching

1. In the will and providence of the Lord, women give birth, despite sorrow in childbirth due to the curse.

   - *Matthew 11:11 Verily I say unto you, Among them that are born of women there hath not risen a greater than John the Baptist: notwithstanding he that is least in the kingdom of heaven is greater than he.*

2. The greatest birth was the birth of the Messiah.

   - *Luke 1:28 And the angel came in unto her [Mary], and said, Hail, thou that art highly favoured, the Lord is with thee: blessed art thou among women.*

3. While Mary was blessed among women she was not blessed above them to the point of deification or worship.

   - *Luke 1:42 And she [Elizabeth] spake out with a loud voice, and said [to Mary], Blessed art thou among women, and blessed is the fruit of thy womb.*

4. During the ministry of Christ, when He fed the multitudes He fed both men and women and the children. Such is the compassion of His heart.

   - *Matthew 14:21 And they that had eaten were about five thousand men, beside women and children.*

   - *Matthew 15:38 And they that did eat were four thousand men, beside women and children.*

5. In prophetic language Jesus foretold the great tribulation and used women hard at work by way of illustration.

   - *Matthew 24:41 Two women shall be grinding at the mill; the one shall be taken, and the other left.*

6. Women followed Christ throughout His public earthly ministry in order to take care of His needs.

- *Matthew 27:55 And many women were there beholding afar off, which followed Jesus from Galilee, ministering unto him:*

- *Mark 15:41 (Who also, when he was in Galilee, followed him, and ministered unto him ;) and many other women which came up with him unto Jerusalem.*

7. Godly women followed Christ to the Cross with tears.

- *Luke 23:27 And there followed him a great company of people, and of women, which also bewailed and lamented him.*

8. Godly women lingered at the foot of the Cross while Jesus died.

- *Mark 15:40 There were also women looking on afar off: among whom was Mary Magdalene, and Mary the mother of James the less and of Joses, and Salome;*

- *Luke 23:49 And all his acquaintance, and the women that followed him from Galilee, stood afar off, beholding these things.*

9. Godly women watched to see where Christ was buried.

- *Luke 23:55 And the women also, which came with him from Galilee, followed after, and beheld the sepulchre, and how his body was laid.*

10. Women were the first to be at the tomb on resurrection morning, the first to be told Christ was alive, the first to behold the resurrected Christ and the first to inform others. What a place of honor they hold in church history.

- *Matthew 28:5 And the angel answered and said unto the women, Fear not ye: for I know that ye seek Jesus, which was crucified.*

- *Luke 24:10 It was Mary Magdalene, and Joanna, and Mary the mother of James, and other women that were with them, which told these things unto the apostles.*

- *Luke 24:24 And certain of them which were with us [such as Peter and John] went to the sepulchre, and found it even so as the women had said: but him [Jesus] they saw not.*

11. One reason why the women were present at the Cross and at the grave site on resurrection morning is because of the miracle of redeeming grace they had experienced. One example is that of Mary, called Magdalene.

- *Luke 8:2 And certain women, which had been healed of evil spirits and infirmities, Mary called Magdalene, out of whom went seven devils,*

12. On the day of Pentecost godly women were found with the apostles in prayer waiting for the promise of the power of the Holy Spirit.

- *Acts 1:14 These all continued with one accord in prayer and supplication, with the women, and Mary the mother of Jesus, and with his brethren.*

13. Following the outpouring of the Spirit on the Day of Pentecost the Lord added to the church on a daily basis men and women who believed the gospel and were converted.

- *Acts 5:14 And believers were the more added to the Lord, multitudes both of men and women.)*

14. As women shared in gospel privileges such as personal salvation, healing miracles, prayer, and receiving the power from on high so they shared in the hardships and persecution of the gospel.

- *Acts 8:3 As for Saul, he made havock of the church, entering into every house, and haling men and women committed them to prison.*

- *Acts 22:4 And I [as Saul of Tarsus] persecuted this way unto the death, binding and delivering into prisons both men and women.*

15. Despite the threat of suffering women continued to come to Christ for salvation.

- *Acts 8:12 But when they believed Philip preaching the things concerning the kingdom of God, and the name of Jesus Christ, they were baptized, both men and women.*

- *Acts 9:2 And desired of him letters to Damascus to the synagogues, that if he found any of this way, whether they were men or women, he might bring them bound unto Jerusalem.*

- *Acts 13:50 But the Jews stirred up the devout and honourable women, and the chief men of the city, and raised persecution against Paul and Barnabas, and expelled them out of their coasts.*

16. The apostles were not opposed to ministering exclusively to women if the opportunity arose.

- *Acts 16:13 And on the Sabbath we went out of the city by a river side, where prayer was wont to be made; and we sat down, and spake unto the women which resorted thither.*

17. God honors specialized ministry to women.

- *Acts 17:4 And some of them believed, and consorted with Paul and Silas; and of the devout Greeks a great multitude, and of the chief women not a few.*

18. The gospel saves women of all ages and nationalities.

- *Acts 17:12 Therefore many of them believed; also of honourable women which were Greeks, and of men, not a few.*

19. Some women can and do commit the most vile of offenses towards God including the sin of lesbianism.

- *Romans 1:26 For this cause God gave them up unto vile affections: for even their women did change the natural use into that which is against nature:*

20. In the church of Corinth when the women began to become disruptive in the service Paul had to write to tell them to be silent during worship.

- *1 Corinthians 14:34 Let your women keep silence in the churches: for it is not permitted unto them to speak; but they are commanded to be under obedience, as also saith the law.*

- *1 Corinthians 14:35 And if they will learn any thing, let them ask their husbands at home: for it is a shame for women to speak in the church.*

21. In the dissemination of the gospel Paul speaks of those women who labored with him in advancing the cause of Christ.

- *Philippians 4:3 And I intreat thee also, true yokefellow, help those women which laboured with me in the gospel, with Clement also, and with other my fellowlabourers, whose names are in the book of life.*

22. When some women in the church were not being as modest as they might nor as humble as the riches of God's material grace allowed, Paul reminded them of how they should act.

- *1 Timothy 2:9 In like manner also, that women adorn themselves in modest apparel, with shamefacedness and sobriety; not with broided hair, or gold, or pearls, or costly array;*

23. Ladies of redeeming grace should always be characterized by good works.

- *1 Timothy 2:10 But (which becometh women professing godliness) with good works.*

24. It was apostolic concern that caused Paul to remind the church to respect all women. The older ladies in the congregation are to be regarded as mothers while the younger women are to be treated in the same manner a man would want someone to treat his sister.

- *1 Timothy 5:2 The elder women as mothers; the younger as sisters, with all purity.*

25. In the context of who should be supported by the church for economic reasons Paul gives his personal pastoral counsel. It does not seem to have the same universal force as a *"Thus saith the Lord."*

- *1 Timothy 5:14 I will therefore that the younger women marry, bear children, guide the house, give none occasion to the adversary to speak reproachfully.*

On another occasion when it seems he is giving his pastoral counsel on a matter Paul adds that he believes he does have the mind of the Spirit of God.

- *1 Corinthians 7:40 But she is happier if she so abide, after my judgment: and I think also that I have the Spirit of God.*

By way of a personal note, I believe it is possible for a Christian mother who works to *"marry, bear children, guide the house, give none occasion to the adversary to speak reproachfully."* I have watched my wife do this for the past twenty-eight years.

26. It is possible for women with too much time on their hands to be led astray into sin.

- *2 Timothy 3:6 For of this sort are they which creep into houses, and lead captive silly women laden with sins, led away with divers lusts,*

27. The older women have a responsibility to the younger women in the church to teach them godliness by practice and then by precept.

- *Titus 2:3 The aged women likewise, that they be in behaviour as becometh holiness, not false accusers, not given to much wine, teachers of good things;*

- *Titus 2:4 That they may teach the young women to be sober, to love their husbands, to love their children,*

It is instructive that women must be taught to love their husbands, especially in arranged marriages, and to love their children, for maternal love is not as natural as might be expected. The abortion industry proves this to be true.

28. Great faith produces great results in ladies of grace.

- *Hebrews 11:35 Women received their dead raised to life again: and others were tortured, not accepting deliverance; that they might obtain a better resurrection:*

29. Christian women who understand the divine order of creation and the need for a final spiritual authority in the home can received the doctrine of submission with a happy heart.

- *1 Peter 3:5 For after this manner in the old time the holy women also, who trusted in God, adorned themselves, being in subjection unto their own husbands:*

30. In the book of the *Revelation* unusual creatures have long lovely hair such is found on a woman of great youth and beauty but hideous teeth.

- *Revelation 9:8 And they had hair as the hair of women, and their teeth were as the teeth of lions.*

31. In the Jewish economy intimacy could make a person ceremonially unclean for worship, which is probably what is in view in Revelation 14:4.

- *Revelation 14:4 These are they which were not defiled with women; for they are virgins. These are they which follow the Lamb whithersoever he goeth. These were redeemed from among men, being the firstfruits unto God and to the Lamb.*

SONG OF SOLOMON 7

Solomon

1 How beautiful are thy feet with shoes, O prince's daughter! The joints of thy thighs are like jewels, the work of the hands of a cunning workman.

7:1 How beautiful. Once more Solomon returns to describing the ravishing physical beauty of the Shulamite maiden in eleven particulars.

- Feet
- Thighs
- Navel
- Belly
- Breasts
- Neck
- Eyes
- Nose
- Head
- Hair
- Roof of the mouth

In chapter 4 the maiden had been described following an espousal to her lover; in this chapter the maiden is described following an interruption in fellowship. The larger point being the consistency of the lover. In like manner Christ has proven He will love His own to the end and establish them in holiness (1 Thess. 3:13).

Matthew Henry Comments on Each Bodily Part and its Spiritual Significance

7:1 feet. Her feet are here praised; the feet of Christ's ministers are beautiful in the eyes of the church (Isaiah 52:7), and her feet are here said to be beautiful in the eyes of Christ. How beautiful are thy feet with shoes! When believers, being made free from the captivity of sin (Acts 12:8), stand fast in the liberty with which they are made free, preserve the tokens of their enfranchisement, have their feet shod with the preparation of the gospel of peace, and walk steadily according to the rule of the gospel, then their feet are beautiful with shoes; they tread firmly, being well armed against the troubles they meet with in their way. When we rest not in good affections, but they are accompanied with sincere endeavors and resolutions, then our feet are beautified with shoes. See Ezekiel 16:10.

7:1 thighs. The joint of the thighs are here said to be like jewels, and those curiously wrought by a cunning workman. This is explained by Ephesians 4:16 and Colossians 2:19, where the mystical body of Christ is said to be held together by joints and bands, as the hips and knees (both which are the joints of the thighs) serve the natural body in its strength and motion. The church is then comely in Christ's eyes when those joints are kept firm by holy love and unity, and the communion of saints. When believers act in religion from good principles, and are steady and regular in their whole conversation, and turn themselves easily to every duty in its time and place, then the joints are like jewels.

2 Thy navel *is like* a round goblet, *which* wanteth not liquor: thy belly *is like* an heap of wheat set about with lilies.

7:2 navel. The navel is here compared to a round cup or goblet, that wants not any of the agreeable liquor that one would wish to find in it, such as David's cup that ran over (Psalms 23:5), well shaped, and not as that miserable infant whose navel was not cut, Ezekiel 16:4. The fear of the Lord is said to be health to the navel. See Proverbs 3:8. When the soul wants not that fear then the navel wants not liquor.

7:2 belly. The belly is like a heap of wheat in the store-chamber, which perhaps was sometimes, to make show, adorned with flowers. The wheat is useful, the lilies are beautiful; there is every thing in the church which may be to the members of that body either for use or for ornament. All the body is nourished from the belly; it denotes the spiritual prosperity of a believer and the healthful constitution of the soul all in good plight.

3 Thy two breasts *are* like two young roes *that are* twins.

7:3 two breasts. By the breasts of the church's consolations those are nourished who are born from its belly (Isaiah 46:3), and by the navel received nourishment in the womb. This comparison we had before, SOS 4:5,

4 Thy neck *is* as a tower of ivory; thine eyes *like* the fish pools in Heshbon, by the gate of Bathrabbim: thy nose *is* as the tower of Lebanon which looketh toward Damascus.

7:4 neck. The neck, which before was compared to the tower of David (SOS 4:4), is here compared to a tower of ivory, so white, so precious; such is the faith of the saints, by which they are joined to Christ their head. The name of the Lord, improved by faith, is to the saints as a strong and impregnable tower.

7:4 eyes. The eyes are compared to the fish-pools for they are clear, deep, quiet, and full reflecting the image of the heavenly Bridegroom. In the Revelation we read of how John was shown a pure river of water of life *"clear as crystal, proceeding out of the throne of God and of the Lamb" (Revelation 22:1).*

By way of personal application, the understanding and the intentions of a believer should be as clean and clear as these ponds. The eyes, weeping for sin, are as fountains (Jeremiah 9:1), and they are comely or lovely in the sight of Christ. Heshbon was east of Jordan and once the residence of the Amorite king Sihon (Numbers 21:25 etc.), afterward held by Gad.

7:4 nose. The nose is like the tower of Lebanon, the forehead or face set like a flint (Isaiah 50:7), undaunted as that tower was impregnable. So it denotes the magnanimity and holy bravery of the church or (as others) a spiritual sagacity [wisdom] to discern things that differ, as animals strangely distinguish by the smell. This tower looks towards Damascus, the head city of Syria, denoting the boldness of the church in facing its enemies and not fearing them (M. Henry).

7:4 Heshbon (hesh'-bon; prudence; stronghold), is used in a figurative way. There were bright pools in the stream which runs beneath Heshbon on the W. The eyes of the Shulamite are said to be like the *"fish pools of Heshbon,"* by the gate of Bath-rabbim.

7:4 Bath-Rabbim (bath-rab'-bim; daughter of many), was one of the gates of Heshbon. The pools nearby were compared in a favorable way to the eyes of the one who was loved.

7:4 Lebanon (le-ba'-na; white), refers to a snow capped mountain range of Syria which forms the N boundary of the land of Palestine (Deut. 1:7; Josh. 1:4).

5 Thine head upon thee *is* like Carmel, and the hair of thine head like purple; the king *is* held [enslaved] in the galleries.

7:5 head. The head like Carmel, a very high hill near the sea, v. 5. The head of a believer is lifted up above his enemies (Psalms 27:6), above the storms of the lower region, as the top of Carmel was, pointing heaven-ward. The more we get above this world, and the nearer to heaven, and the more secure and serene we become by that means, the more amiable we are in the eyes of the Lord Jesus (M. Henry).

7:5 hair. The hair of the head is said to be like purple. This denotes the universal amiableness of a believer in the eyes of Christ, even to the hair, or (as some understand it) the pins with which the hair is dressed. Some by the head and the hair understand the governors of the church, who, if they be careful to do their duty, add much to her comeliness. The head like crimson (so some read it) and the hair like purple, the two colors worn by great men (M. Henry).

7:5 Carmel (car'-mel; the park; fruit garden, orchard), was located in the hill country of Judah (Josh. 15:55). It was located 8 miles SE of Hebron.

6 How fair and how pleasant art thou, O love, for delights!

7 This thy stature is like to a palm tree, and thy breasts to clusters *of grapes.*

8 I said, I will go up to the palm tree, I will take hold of the boughs [branches] thereof: now also thy breasts shall be as clusters of the vine, and the smell of thy nose like apples;

7:8 palm trees. He [Solomon] compares her stature to a palm-tree, so straight, so strong, does she appear, when she is looked upon in her full proportion. The palm-tree is observed to flourish most when it is loaded; so the church, the more it has been afflicted, the more it has multiplied; and the branches of it are emblems of victory. Christ says, *"I will go up to the palm-tree, to entertain myself with the shadow of it (v. 8) and I will take hold of its boughs and observe the beauty of them"* What Christ has said he will do, in favour to his people; we may be sure he will do it, for his kind purposes are never suffered to fall to the ground; and if he take hold of the boughs of his church, take early hold of her branches, when they are young and tender, he will keep his hold and not let them go (M. Henry).

9 And the roof of thy mouth like the best wine for my beloved, that goeth *down* sweetly, causing the lips of those that are asleep to speak.

7:7-9. [Solomon speaks of how he will go] to refresh himself with her fruits. He compares her breasts (her pious affections towards him) to clusters of grapes, a most pleasant fruit (v. 7), and he repeats it (v. 8): They shall be (that is, they shall be to me) as clusters of the vine, which make glad the heart. *"Now that I come up to the palm-tree thy graces shall be exerted and excited."* [Spiritually] Christ's presence with his people kindles the holy heavenly fire in their souls, and then their breasts shall be as clusters of the vine, a cordial to themselves and acceptable to him. And since God, at first, breathed into man's nostrils the breath of life, and breathes the breath of the new life still, the smell of their nostrils is like the smell of apples, or oranges, which is pleasing and reviving. The Lord smelt a sweet savour from Noah's sacrifice, Genesis 8:21. And, lastly, the roof of her mouth is like the best wine (v. 9); her spiritual taste and relish, or the words she speaks of God and man, which come not from the teeth outward, but from the roof of the mouth, these are pleasing to God. The prayer of the upright is his delight. And, when those that fear the Lord speak one to another as becomes them, the Lord hearkens, and hears with pleasure, Malachi 3:16. It is like that wine which is very palatable and grateful to the taste. It goes down sweetly; *it goes straightly* (so the margin reads it); *it moves itself aright,* Proverbs 23:31. The pleasures of sense seem right to the carnal appetite, and go down smoothly, but they are often wrong, and, compared with the pleasure of communion with God, they are harsh and rough. Nothing goes down so sweetly with a gracious soul as the wine of God's consolations (M. Henry).

The Shulamite Maiden

10 I *am* my beloved's, and his desire *is* toward me.

7:10 his desire is toward me. Like Solomon the heart of the Savior is not turned from those for whom He has died. The Christian can take hope.

> "Oh, I am my Beloved's,
>   And my Beloved's mine,
> He brings a poor vile sinner
>   Into His house of wine;
>
> I stand upon His merit,
>   I know no safer stand,
> Not e'en where glory dwelleth
>   In Immanuel's land."
>
> Rutherford

11 Come, my beloved, let us go forth into the field; let us lodge [rest] in the villages.

12 Let us get up early to the vineyards; let us see if the vine flourish, *whether* the tender grape appear [open]], *and* the pomegranates bud forth: there will I give thee my loves.

7:11-12 come. Having received fresh tokens of abiding faithfulness the Shulamite maiden is anxious to respond to love. In like manner the goodness of God in grace is designed to lead the heart to repent of sin and live a more holy life. *Romans 2:4 Or despisest thou the riches of his goodness and forbearance and longsuffering; not knowing that the goodness of God leadeth thee to repentance?*

13 The mandrakes give a smell, and at our gates *are* all manner of pleasant *fruits,* new and old, *which* I have laid up for thee, O my beloved.

7:13 mandrakes. The Hebrew word signifies *"love plants."* The mandrakes are associated with increasing a person's sexuality (Gen. 30:14). The plant grows in the valley of Jordan and along the waters running into the Jordan, in the plains of Moab and Gilead. The mandrake appearance is that of lettuce with wavy dark green leaves. The flowers are violet, white, or deep blue. In early May a fruit appears resembling a small tomato and gives a pleasant odor to the Orientals. The fruit is good to eat. The Arabs refer to the fruit as *"devil's apple."* Mandrakes were also used as a narcotic.

SONG OF SOLOMON 8

The Shulamite Maiden's Love for Solomon
and the Church's Love for Christ

1 O that thou wert as my brother, that sucked the breasts of my mother! *When* I should find thee without, I would kiss thee; yea, I should not be despised.

8:1 find thee without. The maiden declares she wants to show a more open love for Solomon and kiss him much like she would shower a nursing baby brother with kisses. The church must find ways to openly confess her love for Christ and not be ashamed.

2 I would lead thee, *and* bring thee into my mother's house, *who* would instruct me: I would cause thee to drink of spiced wine of the juice of my pomegranate.

8:2 instruct me. Either the maiden wants to be instructed in what pleases Solomon as she shows him her house or she is willing to be instructed by her mother on how to please a husband. In either case the Church must be willing to be taught of Christ. Indeed, He has come that he might give us an understanding.

8:2 pomegranate, refers to a round, red, juicy fruit with a hard rind and numerous seeds (Num. 20:5; Deut. 8:8; Song of Sol. 4:13). The maiden says she will cause Solomon to drink of the best she has. So the church should give of her best to the Master.

"Give of your best to the Master;
Give of the strength of your youth.
Throw your soul's fresh, glowing ardor
Into the battle for truth.

Jesus has set the example,
Dauntless was He, young and brave.
Give Him your loyal devotion;
Give Him the best that you have.

Give of your best to the Master;
Give of the strength of your youth.

Clad in salvation's full armor,
Join in the battle for truth.

Give of your best to the Master;
Give Him first place in your heart.
Give Him first place in your service;
Consecrate every part.

Give, and to you will be given;
God His beloved Son gave.
Gratefully seeking to serve Him,
Give Him the best that you have.

Give of your best to the Master;
Naught else is worthy His love.
He gave Himself for your ransom,
Gave up His glory above.

Laid down His life without murmur,
You from sin's ruin to save.

Give Him your heart's adoration;
Give Him the best that you have."

Howard B. Grouse (1851-1939)

3 His left hand *should be* under my head, and his right hand should embrace me.

4 I charge you, O daughters of Jerusalem, that ye stir not up, nor awake *my* love, until he please.

The Daughters of Jerusalem

5 Who *is* this that cometh up from the wilderness [desert], leaning upon her beloved?
Solomon Speaks

I raised [awakened] thee up under the apple tree: [and as they drew near the home of the Shulamite maiden Solomon pointed and said] there thy mother brought thee forth [conceived thee]: there she brought thee forth [was in labor] *that* bare thee.

8:2 apple tree (tappuwach [tap-poo'-akh]). The reference may indicate the apricot, a native of China that was introduced into Mesopotamia and Palestine prior to the days of Abraham. The favorable climate can cause this tree with spreading branches to grow to 30ft.in height. It may be that the apricot was the *"forbidden fruit"* of the Garden of Eden.

The Shulamite Maiden Pleads Never to be Forgotten

6 Set me as a seal upon thine heart, as a seal upon thine arm: for love *is* strong as death; jealousy is cruel as the grave: the coals thereof *are* coals of fire, which *hath* a most vehement flame.

8:6 as a seal. The seal speaks of something confirmed and settled. When a legal document is drawn up, the contents are sealed and settled. Spiritually, every believer is sealed with the Holy Spirit of promise (Eph. 1:13).

Four Characteristics of Love

- Love has strength. *"Love is strong as death."*
- Love is jealous which in context means love is firm or unyielding.
- Love is enduring. *"Many waters cannot quench love, neither can the floods drown it."*
- Love has value. *"If a man would give all the substance of his house for love, it would utterly be contemned."*

---

7 Many waters cannot quench love, neither can the floods drown it: if *a* man would give all the substance of his house for love, it would utterly be contemned.

The Brothers of the Shulamite

8 We have a little sister, and she hath no breasts: what shall we do for our sister in the day when she shall be spoken for?

9 If she *be* a wall [chaste and pure], we will build upon her a palace of silver: and if she *be* a door [loose and immoral], we will inclose her with boards of cedar.

8:8-9 she hath no breasts. The brothers of the Shulamite did not appreciate her nor have hopes of her maturing and becoming marriageable. To their surprise she captured the heart of the king. In like manner, the church appears contemptible in the eyes of the world. But she has captured the heart of the King of kings and Lord of lords.

The Shulamite Maiden Responds

10 I *am* a wall, and my breasts like towers: then was I in his eyes as one that found favour.

The Daughters of Jerusalem

11 Solomon had a vineyard at Baal-hamon; he let out the vineyard unto keepers; every one for the fruit thereof was to bring a thousand *pieces* of silver.

8:11 Solomon (sol'-o-mun; peaceful), was the son of David and third king of Israel. Following his reign the United Kingdom divided so that there was the southern kingdom of Judah and the Northern Kingdom of Israel.

8:11 Baal-Hamon (ba"-al-ha'-mon; lord of the multitude; who rules a crowd), refers to the location of a vineyard of Solomon in the northern country of Ephraim.

The Shulamite Maiden

12 My vineyard, which *is* mine, *is* before me: thou, O Solomon, *must have* a thousand [pieces of silver], and those that keep the fruit thereof two hundred.

8:12 must have. Love gives. While Solomon does not need the money from the maiden's vineyard she wants to give to him as he will give to her. Spiritually, the Lord bestows great wealth upon His people and His gifts are without repentance.

Solomon

13 Thou that dwellest in the gardens, the companions hearken [listen] to thy voice: cause me to hear it.

14 Make haste, my beloved, and be thou like to a roe or to a young hart upon the mountains of spices.

8:14 make haste. The narrative ends with a magical moment of romantic passion. There is a holy eagerness to be together for ever and ever. Even so the church says to Christ, *"Come quickly, Lord Jesus."*

Thirteen Questions Asked in the Song of Solomon

1. *Song of Solomon 1:7 Tell me, O thou whom my soul loveth, where thou feedest, where thou makest thy flock to rest at noon: for why should I be as one that turneth aside by the flocks of thy companions?*

2. *Song of Solomon 3:3 The watchmen that go about the city found me: to whom I said, Saw ye him whom my soul loveth?*

3. *Song of Solomon 3:6 Who is this that cometh out of the wilderness like pillars of smoke, perfumed with myrrh and frankincense, with all powders of the merchant?*

4. *Song of Solomon 5:3 I have put off my coat; how shall I put it on?*

5. *Song of Solomon 5:3 I have washed my feet; how shall I defile them?*

6. *Song of Solomon 5:9 What is thy beloved more than another beloved, O thou fairest among women?*

7. *Song of Solomon 5:9 What is thy beloved more than another beloved, that thou dost so charge us?*

8. *Song of Solomon 6:1 Whither is thy beloved gone, O thou fairest among women?*

9. *Song of Solomon 6:1 Whither is thy beloved turned aside? That we may seek him with thee.*

10. *Song of Solomon 6:10 Who is she that looketh forth as the morning, fair as the moon, clear as the sun, and terrible as an army with banners?*

11. *Song of Solomon 6:13 Return, return, O Shulamite; return, return, that we may look upon thee. What will ye see in the Shulamite? As it were the company of two armies.*

12. *Song of Solomon 8:5 Who is this that cometh up from the wilderness, leaning upon her beloved? I raised thee up under the apple tree: there thy mother brought thee forth: there she brought thee forth that bare thee.*

13. *Song of Solomon 8:8 We have a little sister, and she hath no breasts: what shall we do for our sister in the day when she shall be spoken for?*

For additional writings by Stanford E. Murrell, visit his website at:

www.stanmurrell.org

Made in the USA
Middletown, DE
05 July 2020